The Thirst of God

The Thirst of God

Contemplating God's Love with Three Women Mystics

Wendy Farley

WJK Westminster John Knox Press
Louisville • Kentucky

First edition
Published by Westminster John Knox Press
Louisville, Kentucky

15 16 17 18 19 20 21 22 23 24—10 9 8 7 6 5 4 3 2 1

Book design by Sharon Adams
Cover design by Allison Taylor

Library of Congress Cataloging-in-Publication Data

Farley, Wendy, 1958-
The thirst of God : contemplating God's love with three women mystics / Wendy Farley.
pages cm
ISBN 978-0-664-25986-0 (alk. paper)
1. Mysticism. 2. Love--Religious aspects--Christianity. 3. God (Christianity)--Love. 4. God (Christianity)--Worship and love. 5. Spiritual life--Catholic Church. 6. Mechthild, of Magdeburg, approximately 1212-approximately 1282. 7. Porete, Marguerite, approximately 1250-1310. 8. Julian, of Norwich, 1343- I. Title.
BV5082.3.F37 2015
248.2'209252--dc23

2015002759

♾ The paper used in this publication meets the minimum requirements of the American National Standard for Information Sciences—Permanence of Paper for Printed Library Materials, ANSI Z39.48-1992.

To Liz—
whose dancing and wise spirit has been an incalculable joy throughout my life

And to my mother, Doris, a light of love to me as to many others

Contents

A Note to Readers and Acknowledgments

A few words about the kind of book this is and the kind of readers who might be interested. The genesis of this book was the many conversations I have had over the years with dedicated but frustrated Christians who are in the church, at the margins of the church, or who have abandoned it altogether. For them, I would like to send a word of solidarity and say that there is a rich tradition of wonderful women and other contemplatives who are great resources for thinking differently about Christianity. They emphasize divine love, human compassion, and the radical possibilities of contemplative practices. They were not afraid to criticize the church and indeed thought of their challenge as crucial to their faith. We do not have to lose faith in the beautiful wisdom of this story of intimate and compassionate love dwelling among us and within us.

I also teach theology at a university and am inspired by the way the borders of theology are constantly expanding and becoming more inclusive. I hope that people studying and teaching theology will widen their scope still further by including these amazing women on their reading lists. They merit a place next to Gregory of Nyssa, Augustine, and Luther. Like other great theologians, they challenge our assumptions and demand that we expand our sense of what counts as the written body of Christ.

These women do not write in scholastic or systematic style. Their theology is like that of the Bible or of Dante or Coleridge. It emerges from image, dialogue, exemplum. In interpreting the theology and spirituality of these women we need to learn how to read images theologically. I have attempted to do this here, to get at the theological meaning and significance of these women by paying close attention to the different genres of their writing. This does not make them less theologically sophisticated than academically trained male theologians, but it does challenge us to new methods of interpretation.

All three women are contemplatives, and two of them record visionary experiences. I do not think this genre should distress contemporary readers. In the medieval period, it was the only form in which women could hope to be taken seriously. Marguerite Porete's refusal to write in this way is one of the reasons she was executed. It is sad irony that the very thing that granted them a voice in one period of history condemns them to the outer borders of serious thinking in our own. We do not need a theory of visions or even religious experience to read them. Simply taking the images on their own terms and working with them theologically is sufficient to allow us access to their profound wisdom.

What we believe translates into what we do and how we construct our societies. These women were ardent lovers of God and bracing critics of the theological assumptions that have shaped much of Christian history. Writing about love as the central attribute of God was not a private, subjective, feminine, navel-gazing bit of "mystical" experience. It is a dramatic challenge to the social and religious apotheosis of the logic of domination and patriarchy that tears humanity into segments, some worthy of salvation, others not. I have read these women not only for their great spiritual and theological insights but because their contemplative theology is also political theology. If it were not, they would not have experienced the conflict they did. Taking them seriously as theologians has meant for me thinking more carefully about the way theologians of the classical tradition may have colluded with political regimes that governed by ideological control and violence.

I have tried to write in a way that is scholastically responsible without distracting readers who are not professional academics. My footnotes give basic credit to the secondary literature to which I am indebted. I am including a bibliography that will prove a useful resource for readers interested in further study.

The translations of the three primary texts I am using are my own. I am not an expert in any of these languages and would not encourage readers to prefer my translations to others. I worked from the texts in each original language and consulted several English translations. I hope I have captured enough of their meaning in my admittedly amateurish translations. I did very much enjoy their fascinating and often untranslatable imagery, puns, and strange words. Who could fail to appreciate Julian's "dear-worthy" lovers of God or be startled by Marguerite's strange term for the soul that held back nothing from God—adnientie: annihilated? Nothinged? Made nothing? And yet in a way that is inebriated with joy.

I hope my very brief introduction to these "dear-worthy" women who were "reduced to nothing" by their inebriation in divine Love may entice readers to pick up one of their books. I hope my readers discover for themselves the sweet mystery that enlarged these women's hearts and gave them the courage to pick up their pens and write for us. They suffered much because of the absence of guides in the way of Divine Lady Love and endangered themselves so that others would not feel so alone. May the recovery of their texts speak to another generation of "God-hunting hearts."

I am grateful to the Louisville Institute and Emory University for funds that allowed me to take a leave to finish this book. I am grateful to the women and men in retreats and study groups that have been curious about these women and inspired me to provide a simple introduction. I am grateful to colleagues who constantly press me toward clearer thinking. I am grateful to the many generations of graduate and undergraduate students who have wrestled with these texts, not least those who have gone on to publish more sophisticated books than this one about women theologians (Emily Holmes, Min Ah Cho, Michelle Voss Roberts, Shelly Rambo, Marcia Mount Shoop, Elizabeth Gandolfo). I thank my older daughter, Emma, for her help with Mechthild's confusing German, even when our communication had to be carried out between Atlanta and a tiny village in Mozambique. I thank my younger daughter, Yana, for her stimulating theological conversation and doing all those dishes I left in the sink. I thank my son, Paul, for prodding my thinking by sharing his own reflections in papers he has written on Buddhist thought and practice. I am grateful to Beth Waltemath, Bev Eliot, and my sister, Amy Howe, who teach me so much about what the church can look like when it is ministered to by women. I am grateful to WJK and its editors, especially Robert Ratcliff, Julie Tonini, and Daniel Braden for supporting yet another of my theological efforts.

Introduction

> "I once was enclosed in the serfdom of prison . . . . Now divine light has delivered me from prison and joined me by gentleness to the divine will of Love, where the Trinity gives me the delight of his love."[1]

Marguerite Porete concluded her magnificent book with this song of freedom. Soon afterward, she was enclosed in a physical prison from which she was led away to be burned as a relapsed heretic. The primary goal of this book is to reintroduce Marguerite, together with Mechthild of Magdeburg and Julian of Norwich, to readers who may never have heard of them. I feel compelled to do this because in this moment of history we are desperate to reawaken the good news that God is love.

These women portray with singular vividness the longing of the divine Love for humanity. Like them, we might believe that it was because of the longing of God for humanity—all of humanity—that divine reality clothed itself in human nature. As Christians we recognize this in Jesus Christ but, confident that divine Love never leaves her children bereft, we also recognize it in the wisdom of all of the spiritual traditions of the world. Love comes to humanity to reincorporate this broken body back into the divine life. In one sense, we have never left it. But in our brokenness and misery, our cruelties and deceptions, we have forgotten who we are and who it is that holds us in the infinitely tender, eternal, and unchanging power of love.

I have watched my older children turn away from the church in disgust and boredom—a church that nurtured me, rooted my parents and sister in patterns of love and courage, and whose congregations still feed the hungry, protest injustice, and comfort those who grieve. My younger daughter is mocked for her Christian faith on the assumption that she hates gays and lesbians and believes everyone is going to hell. (The irony of mocking the daughter of two mothers for her assumed homophobia is lost on her accusers.) I talk with women who have left the faith, scarred and battered by it. I meet women who feel nurtured by the church but want to know how to deepen their faith. I meet young men who are torn between the ways their childhood faith has wounded them and their passion to serve God. I meet converts to Buddhism who are mystified to discover there is a contemplative strand within Christianity. The wisdom of these ancient women is much needed.

As a child I learned that "they will know we are Christians by our love." I believe my own frustration with the church is rooted in the utter confidence in this love, which I learned from my parents and grandmothers. The women I write about in this book are far from being solitary witnesses to this love, but they are exceptionally clear and bright ones. Adding them to the "cloud of witnesses" in our tradition can only refresh and expand our awareness of the depth of this love that encompasses all of creation and dwells in the cavern of every human heart.

But No One Would Tell Me the Truth about Him

The theological canon that I learned in graduate school and have been teaching for nearly thirty years did not teach me much about divine love. The recitals of my sinfulness in the liturgies of my progressive churches did not awaken my mind to the great beauty and dignity of the human soul or who dwells there or how precious it is.[2] There is much to love in "the tradition," but who was this appalling deity that the brilliant minds of Augustine and Aquinas, Calvin and Luther, described as a god whose chief principles of creation included the predestination of arbitrary portions of humanity to hell as a sign of his justice? Was it a good use of his intellect for Augustine to assure us that God's omnipotence would be sufficient to hold an otherwise finite body over a pit of fire forever?

Working for Amnesty International and living with a mother whose daily work brought her in contact with nightmarish lives of abused children, I wanted to hear more than a story of fall, punishment, and forgiveness. Even as a child, I knew that if God is love, it would be impossible for the people of the world, whose beauty and fragilities were like the flowers of the earth, to be cast into hell. And yet I do not remember encountering any canonical theological text that did not assume that non-Christians, or insufficiently good Christians, or Christians whose doctrine was not sound, or simply people arbitrarily chosen as vessels of wrath would suffer that fate. My professors—love and admiration for whom still inspires me—did not believe this. Their own brilliant, compassionate, and courageous writings testify to a different deity. And yet these early fathers constituted the core of my theological education.

I am a constructive theologian as well as a student and teacher of contemplative practices. I do not usually write books like this one. I have spent several years working on this book because when I discovered these amazing women, I realized that my own spiritual and theological hungers did not separate me from the Christian tradition. To the contrary, I was part of a tradition as old as Christianity itself—as old as Wisdom "without whom nothing was made." I was part of the ancient, if mostly invisible, community of women and men in love with the Beloved but who have felt undernourished by the institutional church.

"I wanted to speak of him because no one would tell me about him when I would have listened gladly [until] Lady Love told me the truth about him."[3] Like Marguerite, I longed for news of divine love. When I discovered other pockets of the tradition—Origen, Gregory of Nyssa, Pseudo-Dionysius, John Scotus Eriugena, Schleiermacher, Tillich, and many others—I knew there was a place for me in Christian theology. But when I discovered these women, I knew I was home. I heard with unparalleled intensity the praises of Lady Love, the sweetness of the dark abyss, and the beauty of the soul made and redeemed for intimacy with this spacious goodness. They are not scholastically trained, and this continues to exclude them from the theological canon. But their lack of scholastic training is their great strength. They write immediately and candidly rather than through the mediations and constraints of lines of authority and academic niceties. Like Marguerite, I want to share their exquisite theology and spirituality with others. I want others to know that this, too, is Christianity, and it is theology. I want others to know "the truth about . . . the one who is all love."[4]

Theologies of Love

Who are these women and why are they gathered here? I tell something of this story in later chapters. But a few words here may orient my readers. Mechthild, Marguerite, and Julian are gathered together in this book as witnesses to the spaciousness and graciousness of the Christian path. There are many others that could be here, but, I admit, I love and admire the writings of these women. For a brief and beautiful moment, women believed they would be allowed to write of their experience and their theology. Mechthild of Magdeburg lived from 1207–1282/94. She was a beguine (a lay contemplative—more about that later) who took up writing at the request of her Dominican confessor. By the end of her life, it seems that certain members of the church were becoming hostile to the beguine way of life. In any case, as an old women she retired to a Cistercian convent in Helfta. Marguerite Porete died in 1310. She seems to have begun her life in the heyday of the beguine movement, surrounded by fellow contemplatives, monastics, and theologians. She was swept up by larger politics that were putting in place the mechanisms of inquisition. Her death extinguished the light of this creative period of women's theology and spirituality. She is both the apex and demise of beguine theology. Julian of Norwich was born in 1342 and disappears sometime after 1429. As an anchoress, Julian resided in a tiny cell, about ten by twelve. Though she was invisible to the world, her writings shone a brilliant light.

The arc of these three women transverses a period of hope and energy, through intense and deadly persecution, to a light that refuses to be entirely extinguished. They are themselves participants in a much longer lineage: Perpetua and Felicity, Macrina, Hildegard of Bingen, St. Clare of Assisi, Hadewijch, Teresa of Avila, Margaret Fell, Jarena Lee, and all the named and unnamed women whose lives and work testify to the refusal of the Holy Spirit to color within the lines of patriarchal institutions.

During the twelfth and thirteenth centuries, Europe was aglow with religious renewal. This took many, sometimes contradictory, forms. What interests us here is the women who were energized by religious devotion and wanted to find ways of life that did not restrict them to convents or motherhood. One such movement was the beguines; but to call it a "movement" implies an organization and structure that it did not have. There is no founder, no creed, no vows. The beguines were women who gathered for prayer, study, charitable works, and meditation. They chose lives of voluntary poverty and chastity to strengthen these activities. While continuing to participate in the sacramental life of the church, they also renewed their spiritual lives through contemplative practices.

Mechthild, Marguerite, and Julian were among the many women who experimented with spiritual practices outside the Benedictine or Cistercian convents that were available to wealthy women with large dowries. Like all women who lived before the nineteenth century, an academic education was forbidden to them. (Women were first admitted to a British university in 1878. Nonetheless they were theologians whose contemplative practice opened to them the book of divine love. Each is unique but they share theological common ground in the pride of place they give to divine Love. Mechthild uses the feminine inflected German word *Minne*—translated "Lady Love"—as one of her main images for God. Marguerite personifies the divine voice who leads the soul to unity with God as "Amour" or "Dame Amour." For Julian, Mother Christ infuses the Trinity with love that creates, restores, and nurtures humanity. God is beyond all images and words. But the feminine bespeaks the divine powerfully and evocatively.

These women also share the optimism that human beings can fully participate in this love. Mechthild relies primarily on the erotic and bridal imagery of the Song of Songs and troubadour poetry to portray the union of the soul with God. Marguerite Porete occasionally uses bridal imagery but more often describes union in terms of the soul's disappearance into divine reality. Her word, *adnientie*, is translated in various ways: reduced to nothing, annihilated, or stripped. She does not mean that personhood becomes nothing; rather, she means that those elements of egocentric desire that separate us from God are reduced to nothing. In this joyous "nothingness," we are opened to the spacious goodness of God. Julian of Norwich describes God as thirst: "It is the thirst of God to have all of humanity drawn within Godself."[5] Like her beguine sisters, she gives us a taste of the radical goodness of God, depicting God's longing for us and our longing for God.

These three women are among the apostles of the gospel truth that when we abide in love we abide in God, for God is love. They understand this abiding to be rooted in the transformation of the human soul into love, a transformation that allows belief and action to radiate this goodness to the world. They not only believed that God is love but also believed Lady Love enables her followers and lovers to become that love. "God became human so that humans can become divine," as Athanasius (the energetic defender of the Nicene Creed) put it centuries before.[6] For these contemplatives, desire is the wound of love that draws us to our divine Beloved and our Beloved to us. In this mutual desire, our deepest selves become available to intimacy with divine reality.

Women Theologians and the Church

Although these women wrote in order to participate in a conversation about theology and practice, their relationship with the church was not an easy one. In this, they may prove interesting sisters to contemporary people whose relationship with the church is also uneasy. Mechthild reports that clerics threatened to burn her book. Marguerite was herself burned; though once her book was separated from her name, it enjoyed a vital afterlife. Julian seemed to have enjoyed some local respect, but her writing voice did not emerge from obscurity for some five hundred years.

All three women understood themselves to be Christian and did not identify with the overt dissent of outspoken critics of the church. They seem to have several strikes against them, nonetheless. They were innovators in writing theology in vernacular (local spoken) languages instead of Latin.[7] As time went on, the vernacular was associated with nonclerical writing, therefore with heresy, and fell under suspicion. In England, the "Lollards" (followers of John Wycliffe and his criticisms of the church) advocated translating the Bible into English. The resounding silence surrounding Julian's text may be related to the association of vernacular writing with the Lollard "heresy."

A second problem is that they unabashedly defined God in terms of love and used feminine metaphors to express the sweetness, intimacy, and reliability of this love. It is not heretical to think of God as love, but to use it to redefine Christian faith produces troubling consequences. Origen's argument that if God is powerful and good, the long arc of endless time would be sufficient to save all humanity, was declared anathema. John Scotus Eriugena was condemned for rejecting the doctrine that God eternally predestines part of humanity for hell and part of humanity for salvation. Anselm seems to find eternal punishment inconsistent with divine mercy but did not have the wherewithal to openly reject it.

It seems strange, but throughout the history of Christianity those who have a particularly clear focus on love have been condemned, silenced, or marginalized. These three women were not condemned for their emphasis on Lady Love and Mother Christ. But the readers they attempted to create through their writing—readers able to embody the depth and goodness of divine love—could not appear. The consistently enacted logic of love could only be an affront to a church whose allegiance was to imperial models of divine and human power.

More damning, they were women.[8] Since many contemporary Christian denominations, including the largest, do not ordain women, it perhaps will not shock us that women have not been accepted as interpreters of Christian thought. Even so, women now contribute a great deal to spiritual and theological writing, retreats, and workshops. Some of our most wonderful ministers are women. Even those denominations that continue to exclude women from leadership have no power to criminalize their writings. But the official silencing of Catholic theologian Elizabeth Johnson reminds us that the church's ability to keep women invisible and inaudible is not a thing entirely of the past.

Although contemporary theology is written in vernacular languages, theologies of love and justice are commonplace, and while women are no longer complete strangers to preaching, teaching, or theology, medieval women still tend to bear the stigma imposed by harsher times. They are rarely included in classes on historical or systematic theology.[9] Mechthild has achieved minor historical interest, but the main translator of her work finds in her writings nothing original.[10] Julian is contained in a cocoon of orthodox and sometimes sentimental piety. Marguerite is still a "heretic," and Philip the Fair remains a "loyal defender of the faith."[11] Churches and seminaries continue to accept it as natural that the feminine body of Christ, figuratively and literally, has had its tongue cut out.[12]

Just Who Is "Orthodox" Here?

Most of this book is an exploration of beautiful and important theology. But to argue that these women's books are important to our basic understanding of Christian thought requires that we rethink what is normative and what is marginal. I am not only suggesting that we expand our canon to include Mechthild, Marguerite, and Julian but also asking us to wonder who are the orthodox and who are the heretics in our story? I propose telling a piece of this story from a somewhat off-kilter point of view.

To entangle ourselves in the Sargasso Sea of thirteenth-century politics would take us far astray. But without understanding something of these events, the condemnation of Marguerite by Philip the Fair and the subsequent silence of theological women will be easy to misunderstand.

Philip was an ambitious king, dedicated to extending France's borders and winning the tug of war with the pope about who would be in charge. In 1309, he managed to move the papacy from Rome to Avignon in order to install a French pope. But this bold political move was only a part of his strategy to monopolize wealth and power.

He engaged in long wars that contributed to the hemorrhaging of money from his treasury. Indebted to Jews, he found it expedient to arrest and then expel them from France in order to take over their property. The Knights Templar, who functioned as bankers for both the papacy and French royalty, held a massive debt against Philip. In 1307 he began a campaign to arrest and torture Templar monks. When some hundreds of Templars mounted a defense of their order, Philip responded by burning fifty-four in a field outside of Paris.[13] The rift this caused with the pope did not change the fact that he had come into possession of their funds.

What has all of this to do with Marguerite? In one sense nothing. She was a contemplative and a theologian. This would seem to place her far from the radar of Philip's machinations. The simplest way to describe the motivations for her execution would be to say that she proved a useful pawn whose death would shore up Philip's much besieged reputation as a "defender of the faith." Marguerite served this purpose because she was both more audacious and more vulnerable than other contemplative women. It seemed suspicious to have a woman wandering around, unsupervised by a husband or the regulations of a walled convent. She was a teacher and apparently a popular one. As Bernard McGinn points out, she was burned in part for failing to observe the limits imposed upon her.[14] After the appalling scandal of the Templars, the show trial of an outspoken beguine would burnish Philip's reputation as a champion of orthodoxy.

Julian of Norwich, born thirty-two years after Marguerite's execution, was symbolically dead and buried in her anchor-hold, and her writings were never widely circulated. But Norwich was honored with its own energetic defender of Christianity in the person of its Bishop, Henry le Despenser ("the Fighting Bishop").

The church was torn by the scandal of having a pope in Avignon and in Rome, a logical sequence from Philip the Fair's removal of the papacy to France. Kingdoms and bishops lined up in support of one or another of the popes as their own interests dictated. Notwithstanding this transparently political agenda, the pope remained the visible sign of Christ on earth and a symbol of the unity of the church. To the extent that Christians took their faith seriously, a Christendom divided between two popes was a disaster.

Henry le Despenser would have been the bishop that gave Julian last rites as she entered the anchor-hold of St. Julian. In 1383 he received permission to initiate a crusade against France in retaliation for their support of the Avignon pope. English royalty supported the crusade as a part of their economic war on the European cloth trade. Soldiers were enticed with indulgences, assurances that their sins and those of their family would be wiped clean. The English were quickly routed, but even lost crusades must be funded by tithes and taxes. Peasants and serfs provided numerous, if impoverished, sources of money required for war, crusade, and extravagant lifestyles. When they rebelled, the brutality with which they were repressed, spear-headed by Norwich's bishop, indicated the determination of church and state to maintain the status quo.

Upon their return to England, the savagery that served soldiers well in war was now directed at local citizens, who were terrorized by soldier-brigands. Citizens' outrage of rampaging (but shriven) soldiers was coupled with anxiety over loved ones who died suddenly in plague, famine, or flood. These juxtapositions of arbitrary salvation and equally wanton condemnation made a mockery of the power of the church to forgive sins. Criticism of the church and repression of this criticism spiraled in a deadly dance.

In England, criticism was spearheaded by John Wycliffe and the Lollard movement. In 1396 Bishop Despenser was given permission to apply the death penalty against religious dissent. "Heretics" began to be burned in Norwich's public square. The introduction into England of the mechanisms of inquisition occurred not far from Julian's quiet anchor-hold.[15] In crusade, war, massacre, and inquisition Bishop Despenser imitated the techniques of the god to whom he was so loyal.

Babylonian Captivity of the Church

The contrast between orthodoxy and heresy structures much of the way the history of Christianity is told. The lovely scholar and sympathetic translator of Marguerite Porete, Ellen Babinsky, takes Philip at his word and describes him as a "pious leader who was genuinely concerned about the fate of the church and who took seriously his title as 'Most Christian King.'"[16] The much less sympathetic, though exquisitely scholarly, translators of another edition of her work acknowledge that medieval methods were certainly savage but add that Marguerite vaunts a "stubborn persistence in her opinions, even when she knew that this could cost her a cruel death. That this assessment may not be unjust...is shown by her persistence in publishing what had already been condemned."[17] It is remarkable that scholars writing in 1999 would assume that burning a woman alive for attempting to promulgate her work, though cruel and even barbaric, makes a kind of theological or institutional sense. But the assumption that Philip's techniques reflect genuine piety or that Marguerite's execution was probably justified indicate how tightly we are held by the assumption that those in power are by definition orthodox and that their victims are "heretics" and perhaps even deserved to die.

Philip the Fair initiated the schism that would divide Western Christianity between popes for one hundred years. He murdered, tortured, and exiled Jews in order to steal their property to fund his wars. He arrested members of an international religious order, tortured them by outrageous methods into confessing the most absurd fantasies of their tormentors. He burned dozens of them alive to take ownership of what amounted to a large European bank. He had two daughters-in-law tortured, flayed, and executed for alleged adultery. He pocketed taxes extracted from a weary population for a crusade to Jerusalem that he (mercifully) never initiated.

Marguerite taught and wrote and prayed. She courageously defended the name of God as love and the capacity of human persons, including women, to fall in love with that love. In contrast to harsh asceticism, she was at pains to offer her fellow beguines a more humane understanding of their practice. As Amy Hollywood argues, her theology "is a direct response to the forms of sanctity prescribed for women . . . and is an attempt to counter a situation of anxiety, struggle, moral rigorism, and bodily suffering."[18] For this she endured eighteen months in an inquisitor's prison and a slow death as flames ate her living flesh.

Orthodoxy means something like "right praise." If we resist construing torture and murder as praise of God, we might recognize Marguerite's tenacity not as "contumacious and rebellious"[19] but as resembling the heroically steadfast faith of Perpetua and Felicity, martyred for their rejection of the theology of Roman imperialism. What if Marguerite was a great Christian martyr and the faith that Philip the Fair and Bishop Despenser defended was not the flickering light of Galilee but a piety they inherited from Roman executioners?

Perpetua, with a slave Felicity, was arrested by Roman officials in 203 CE. She was perhaps twenty-two and had recently given birth to a child. During her imprisonment, she had a dream. She awoke "with the taste of something sweet still in my mouth. I at once told this to my brother, and we realized that we would have to suffer, and that from now on we would no longer have any hope in this life."[20] Like Marguerite, she realized she had fallen into the hands of an utterly implacable power.

Perpetua is a relentless witness to the goodness of God, and her story is heart-wrenching. Her father rages at her stubborn refusal to sacrifice to the emperor—surely a small and empty gesture not worth dying for? Notwithstanding the excruciating compulsions of motherhood and daughterhood, she *could not* accept what passed for piety in Roman religion. The cruelty of its practices and the emptiness of its theology were impossible for her to tolerate. She would not by her actions participate in its theology of death or by her silence renounce the truth she had learned of a God of love. She was obviously a "contumacious and rebellious" traitor to Rome.

The surviving description of her death portrays her going into the stadium with a "shining countenance and calm step, as the beloved of God, as a wife of Christ, putting down everyone's stare by her own intense gaze." After she is first stripped and then gored, she finds herself still alive and waiting for execution by the sword. At this point, she is reported to have said to her fellow Christians, "You must all stand fast in the faith and love one another, and do not be weakened by what we have gone through."

Marguerite is also described as courageous in death. A witness (presumed to be one of those who had condemned her) describes her demeanor as both "noble and pious, in her death. For this reason the faces of many of those who witnessed it were affectionately moved to compassion for her; indeed, the eyes of many were filled with tears."[21]

Marguerite and Perpetua were rebels against empires of violence and their gods. After long months in prison, they still refused to renounce their faith as the price of freedom. It is not accidental that these women who celebrated divine Love and conceived of power in nonimperial symbols were objects of imperial brutality. That is how empires work. They require a theology to underwrite their methods of terror.

What must happen to our Christian faith that we attribute to Philip the Fair an authentic Christian piety and to Marguerite a stubborn and virulent heresy? He acts with the same kind of bloodlust and greed that animated the worst of Rome. She echoes Perpetua's admonition to stand fast in faith and love one another. We might wonder if "orthodox" theology is not implicated in the violence of rulers such as King Philip and Bishop Despenser. Is there a connection between Augustine's insistence that God created most of humanity to be tortured forever in order to display his "justice" and the fires that burned Marguerite? Is there a connection between God's need for payment in blood to restore his honor and Bishop Despenser's crusade and burning "heretics"?

But to leave it there would be to grant to the "powers and principalities" too much. We have these beautiful texts before us and the witness of these courageous women. We have freedom to write, and think, and gather together. We no longer have to fear the physical prisons of Rome or medieval Europe. But we can still inhabit mental prisons. If we have a too narrow understanding of what Christianity can be, then the full reach of the human spirit will be thwarted. But when we begin to explore beyond the narrow confines of an artificially restricted canon and set of beliefs, we find that Christianity is actually very spacious. In it are vast cathedrals for the mind to explore and in which the heart can fly.

As Teresa of Avila says, the soul is like a great diamond with infinite facets. The soul

> is nothing but a paradise in which, as God tells us, He takes his delight [Proverbs 8:31]. . . . I can find nothing with which to compare the great beauty of the soul and its great capacity. . . . For, as He Himself says, He created us in His image and likeness. Now if this is so—and it is—there is no point in our fatiguing ourselves by attempting to comprehend the beauty of this castle [the soul]; for, though it is His creature, and therefore as much difference between it and God as between creator and creature, the very fact that His majesty says it is made in His image means that we can hardly form any conception of the soul's great dignity and beauty.[22]

Mechthild, Marguerite, and Julian cannot exhaust this great mystery and beauty any more than anyone else can. But spending time in their company may be a way for us to begin to taste this "great dignity and beauty" for ourselves.

Prologue

Contemplation of Divine Love

> Clergymen troubled by the Church's frailty repeatedly sought the company of such devout beguines to bolster their own confidence, forming close relationships in which their own alleged deficiencies were offset by the women's special holiness . . . such men admired in religious women what they, their office, and their gender, were perceived to be lacking: true religious poverty, integrity, spontaneity, charisma, a clear presence of the divine, so poignantly absent, many thought, from the institutional Church.[1]

Centuries before the Protestant Reformation, women and other laypeople hungered for more immediate and personal ways to live out the Christian life. Throughout Europe, movements arose advocating simplicity, prayer, and service to the poor and sick. Informally, without direct guidance from bishops or the parish priests, women experimented with practices that would nourish their religious devotion. Beguines and anchoresses were among those who combined contemplative practices with compassionate action and who discovered among themselves a theology of divine love that was not always well represented in the church of the clerics.

We also live in a time of enormous social tumult and change and spiritual creativity. The mainstream denominations struggle, and younger people are likely to consider themselves spiritual but not necessarily religious. Mothers, queers, ministers, single people, and widows again gather in small, informal groups. They go on retreats, learn to meditate, study Scripture, practice compassion, and seek justice. Encountering our sisters from long ago may inspire a thirst for a goodness more beautiful, a compassion more joyous than we knew how to dream.

In the early dawn hours, grey habits move quietly through the pathways of the beguinage to a small chapel. Women gather together and read from Scripture, sing psalms, pray, and sit quietly in meditation. They may be joined by neighborhood women who share their devotion to prayer. Some of these women live with families or alone. Others live with one or two others in houses they share in town. They form a loose community of women who share certain ideals. As dawn breaks, they part.

Small groups leave the beguinage and enter the city. Traveling two or three together, one group goes from house to house in a poor district, ministering to the sick, aiding an overwhelmed woman who has just given birth, encouraging a young woman to get off the street. Another group hires itself out as mourners, imbuing moments of grief with their calm compassion. Others turn their hands to labor, spinning and weaving cloth. Some return to their small cottage and continue to meditate on the readings for the day. Those who enjoy a private income choose a book from a small library. There is a school within the walls where some beguines teach local girls and boys basic literacy and the bones of an education. Virgins and widows live together supporting their way of life with the work of their hands or by begging or through income from family or from those who admire their devotion.[2]

Later in the day, small groups gather again. The literate read aloud to the illiterate from spiritual writings circulating from other contemplatives: beguines, friars, enclosed monks, and nuns. Sometimes they discuss Scripture. The official Bible is the Latin Vulgate; the clergy provide the only official interpretation, and they guard this privilege well. And yet, as lovers of the gospel, contemplative women study Scripture, moved by stories from the gospel and its heroes: the apostles, John the Baptist, Mary Magdalene, Mary the mother of Christ. Images from psalms and prophets enrich their thinking. They discuss prayer and meditation, seeking to unite with the love that flows from the Holy Trinity to humanity. Sometimes they are joined by Dominican or Franciscan monks. Some of these are suspicious of these enterprising women, but many are friends who admire their piety and devotion.

Each woman shapes her activities in ways that suit her vocation. But they share a commitment to prayer, contemplation, and a radical devotion to their Beloved. The increased preoccupation of both the church and society with money, prestige, and power does little to inspire their faith. The bitter feuds and endless wars are troubling contrasts to gospel invitations to charity and love. They, like others in this period, seek spiritual practices focused not on wealth and power but on imitation of Christ and his followers: impoverished but filled with love for God and compassion for the poor and suffering. They try to follow Christ by living simply: wearing a plain gray habit, eating only what is necessary, living without luxury or extravagance. They experiment with ascetic practices such as fasting and prayer vigils. Though some bring children to the community, unmarried or widows, they remain chaste to focus their attention on prayer, study, and service.

These communities have arisen in a period of unusual religious fervor and creativity. They are similar to their counterparts in Italy or southern France: Franciscan tertiaries (Angela of Foligno), Dominican tertiaries (Catherine of Siena), or devoted laywomen (Catherine of Genoa). They blur the edges of rigidly defined social boundaries. They live on the borderlands between lay and religious, scholarly men and "ignorant" women. Many are educated, reading Latin and familiar with theological writings. They sometimes preach, teach, and write but lack the university education and ordination that would authorize these activities. They are laypeople, coming and going in the towns and cities. But their contemplative way of life is similar to that of monastics. They do not live with husbands, but they are not cloistered. They are chaste but have not made permanent vows. They are drawn from different strata of society to live more simply and with greater equality than richly supported nuns. But they have taken no vows of poverty or obedience. Some own their own homes and will them to friends or daughters or sisters. Others live together or in dormitories. Status, in the sense of respect and leadership, accrues from holiness more than from nobility. They are admired for their piety and service and reviled because they are "false women," failing to fit into any of the roles demarcated for them.

Among the beguines we rediscover the finest flowering of women's religious writing of the medieval period. They were among the first to write religious texts in the local language. They were among the most imaginative and bold theologians of their time. Daughters of the church, they anticipated the Protestant emphasis on free access to divine love, a love radically merciful and inclusive. They were drawn to the study of Scripture, but they understood the power of the sacraments and the possibilities of interior prayer. They sought deep intimacy with the divine, whose perfume is evident in their compassionate service and brilliant writing. Though they disappeared behind the silent walls of convent-like beguinages or solitary anchor-holds, their spirited desire continued to resound across time and space in the writings of Teresa of Avila, Simone Weil, Cynthia Bourgeault.

As we experience our own frustrations with church and society, the voices of contemplative women come to us as long-lost sisters and mothers who remind us of the burning light of divine love, piercing any darkness, luminous regardless of the fluctuations of fate. Their lives are models of courage and creativity, and their theologies invite us into depths of the Christian vision that we may hardly know exist. By encountering these women, we become part of this broken lineage of contemplative women that never quite dies. Fragments of this story are told here: in the life and theology of Mechthild of Magdeburg who became a beguine as the movement was getting under way, Marguerite Porete whose execution marked the end of its flourishing, and Julian of Norwich, who was able to carve out a space of freedom unvanquished by fire or fear only by retiring to a shuttered anchor-hold.

PART I

Contemplating Love with Three Women Mystics

1

"Serve Nobly, . . . and Fear Nothing Else"

A Door Opens and Closes: Reigniting Practices of Compassion

"Serve nobly, wish for nothing else, and fear nothing else: and let Love freely take care of herself!"[1]

Perhaps not entirely unlike our own time, the Middle Ages was a period of religious creativity and rapid social and technological change. Opposite impulses flowed through Europe as church and secular leaders struggled for primacy. As Franciscans, beguines, and others fought for the right to practice apostolic poverty, popes, bishops, and kings vied for access to newly created wealth. The church became more authoritarian even as numerous religious movements expanded theological vistas. The threat of purgatory and hell intensified while contemplative women envisioned a theology of love.

The beguines and other contemplative women were among those energized by their ardor for the Holy Beloved to develop new forms of community and practice. Their enthusiasm reflected the sense of possibility that animated this period. But by the turn into the fourteenth century, they became entangled by counterforces that have made "medieval" a watchword for ideological violence.

The beguine movement was surprisingly popular. From a few scattered houses here and there, cottages began to clump together as women were drawn to pray, work, and serve in community with one another. First appearing in Belgium and the Netherlands, this new opportunity for spiritual practice quickly spread to Germany and France. In the early decades of the thirteenth century, the beguinage in Ghent numbered in the thousands. Soon there was hardly a community in the Low Countries without one or more beguinages. But "beguine" does not capture the fluidity of women's religious practices, which included Benedictine or Cistercian convents, enclosed convent-like beguine communities, unenclosed beguines, anchoresses, widows, celibate wives, and women who inhabited different identities at different times. In these informal crosscurrents, women carved out theological insights and spiritual practices that never became fully integrated into the official story of Christianity, but neither did they ever die out completely. Just as a small portion of yeast feeds the whole loaf, the writings of these women witness to God's invitation to humanity to dwell in her divine love and goodness.

Beginnings

Historians can identify the emergence of the beguine way of life as a distinctive vocation. But it appears on the scene without a founder, rule, or beginning moment. Elizabeth of Thuringia's harp player, Aleid, left her position to live a life of penance and contemplation on God's love in 1211. Soon afterward a small community joined her, asking her to act as their spiritual guide.[2] But before Aleid, Mary of Oignies had convinced her husband to live with her celibately. Jacques Vitry relates her story in 1215, indicating she joined an *already existing* community of women and so evidently did not initiate the movement. Features of beguine life can be recognized in the story of her life. Mary's intoxicating love of Christ was seasoned by visions and ecstasies, ascetical practices and work among the outcast, sick, and dying. A group of men and women gathered around her as their teacher. Her combination of contemplative devotion and active ministry became characteristic of many beguines.

Like many men who tell women's stories, Jacques emphasizes her obedience, orthodoxy, and masochistic assaults on her body.[3] He was fascinated by her capacity for visions and ecstasy; her emotional tone was a complement to his own rationalism. Jacques was attracted to these signs of divine nearness but remained preoccupied with harsh penitential practices as the way of accessing this intimacy. We know about the religious life of women mostly through men's writings.[4] Clerics preached about an angry God who required blood atonement. Sin was overwhelming and redemption costly. In response, pious women offered outrageous acts of violent penance.

Men's writings tend to magnify physical suffering, but women could be critical of extreme penitential practices and some discouraged women from self-harm. Beguines' writings modified the theology available to them to reflect more of their own experience. Meditations on the humanity of Christ provoked a sense of the nearness of divine love to suffering humanity. Meditations on the passion became on avenue to participate in divine compassion. The choice of poverty was an implicit criticism of a wealth-infatuated church.

It might seem that asceticism and penance would be acts of self-hatred, but in that time and place, these acts granted women access to their own spiritual power. Asceticism, meditation, and charitable service were elements of divine love experienced and shared.

The Movement Expands

In contrast to those who joined an established religious order, small groups of women gathered around an unofficial leader and advisor (*magistra*) who instructed them in lives of apostolic poverty and contemplation. She might teach literacy to allow them to read the psalms, *lectio divina*, and other devotional literature; she might teach meditation, ascetical practices, charitable works, and in some cases handcrafts to support the community. Very few participants in these practices wrote about them or the theology that percolated in these women's communities. But we are lucky that a few did.

Visions and ecstasies were not outside the norm. Teachers well acquainted with these practices could help discern what visionary experiences were helpful or hurtful, what they understood to be authentic revelations and what were misleading seductions. Our more scientific age is a little bewildered by the idea of visions, but however one interprets them, they are attested to across human cultures and religions. Visionary experience is in part rooted in the practice of visualization and the visual qualities of medieval Christianity. Fasting and sleeplessness can also prime the body for unusual experiences. But it is also the case that the deep wisdom of the human mind, or divine grace (depending on one's point of view), or mature spiritual practice can communicate itself in visual images and imageless insight. Certainly Christians in this period took this for granted.[5]

The authority of teachers did not derive simply from the strangeness of their experiences. There is a charisma of wisdom, discipline, and love that has its own attractiveness. The three most famous beguine theologians, Hadewijch of Brabant, Mechthild of Magdeburg, and Marguerite Porete, appear to have been this kind of leader.

Study and Education

A wide range of education existed among contemplative women. For educated noble women, familiarity with the Latin psalter and at least the rudiments of Latin was not unheard of. Beatrice of Nazareth reportedly could recite all of the psalms in Latin by the age of five. She read Augustine's *De Trinitate* as well as the writings of Hugh and Richard of Saint Victor.[6] Hadewijch of Brabant wrote in Latin as well as Flemish, indicating that her readership included

Latin-reading beguines as well as (possibly) both male and female contemplatives. Familiarity with Latin and availability of small libraries gave access to the writings of Bernard of Clairvaux, William of St. Thierry, and other monastic writers.[7] The beguines' familiarity with troubadour songs and the poetry of courtly love influenced their own thinking. These popular genres portrayed the knight errant, unrequited love, the intensities of erotic desire, and heroic quests. In the writings of women contemplatives the erotic energy and courage of the quest was redirected to describe the boldness of their God-hungry hearts.

As committed as they were to compassionate action, their preferred metaphor for divine love was romantic: less often *caritas* (charity) than *amour* (French) or *minne* (Dutch and German). It was also feminine: Lady Love. Though dedicated to works of charity, romantic love better captured the intensity of their desire and the joy of intimacy with the divine Beloved.

Contemporary readers may find metaphors drawn from the bedroom strange. This may be in part because of the veil that is drawn over sexuality by Puritan forefathers, a veil lifted now by consumerism's crass or exploitative images. Neither of these tempt us to think about a divine Beloved. But as early as the Bible's Song of Solomon, the intense love that we humans feel for the dear one of our heart has seemed a natural way to express the spiritual desire for the mysteriously beautiful and infinitely loving source of our deepest and best longings. To reintroduce ourselves to the spiritual psychology of yearning and the infinite goodness that draws us on can enrich our religious imaginations.[8]

Meditation and Contemplation

During this period of religious change and renewal, contemplative practices gained adherents among the laity; for many, it was a natural component of the apostolic life. They did not think of the apostles only as believers in Jesus but as men and women who imitated his way of life through poverty, prayer, and compassion. They recognized in Jesus' withdrawal for prayer or his admonition to go to a quiet room and pray to the Father in secret (Matt. 6:6) an invitation to contemplative prayer. Meditation is a focused kind of prayer in which the mind concentrates on an image, a word, a passage from Scripture, or an imageless resting in the divine presence. It is a practice that can prepare the heart for transformation by and for love.

One form of meditation practiced by contemplatives was *lectio divina*, a "divine reading." This form of prayer, still popular today, is a way to pass through the external meaning of Scripture to enter its living spirit and allow the grace of the Holy Spirit to enter.[9] Contemplatives were encouraged to enter into a biblical narrative as if they were a part of it. They visualized what it would feel like, what it would smell like, what it would look like to be in the middle of a biblical scene. How would it feel to be Mary Magdalene as she met Jesus for the first time? What "demons" would the contemplative want Jesus to cast out of her: fear, jealousy, distraction, bad memories, hard-heartedness? This kind of meditation forged emotional bonds with Jesus and the saints. It reformed their own emotional patterns so they would be more in line with biblical characters. The compassion of biblical characters would be internalized as compassion for people in the beguine's own community. Contemplation and action, Christ's love for humanity, and the contemplative's love for those around her percolated together. Through meditation, this love would flow into a single river in which desire, will, and action became grounded in the divine love.

Meditation opened a pathway of union with the divine that was inexpressible. The mystery of the divine darkness is the root of the divine love but is impossible to express in language, in visions, or in action. The beguines developed a deep appreciation for the "negative way:" that is, the transcendent mystery of God that defies imagination and eludes all attempts at expression. Doctrine, sacrament, virtue, and Scripture are all routes to the divine life, but they are not identical to God's own being. Contemplative practice brings us to the edge where image and mystery, action and contemplation, darkness and illumination dance together.

A Lively Conversation

The alchemy of theology and practice occurring in women's communities was part of larger discussions among confessors, monks, nuns, friars, and laypeople. Books were read aloud and discussed. Out of these informal conversations emerged a dramatic and rich theology of love. As Robin Anne O'Sullivan puts it, "we might do well to describe beguine communities as a 'school of love.' The women in these communities dedicated themselves to the study of love, God's love and their own, as a way of purifying the 'eyes of the heart.'"[10] Their theological language drew on the erotic imagery of Bernard of Clairvaux's exegesis of the Song of Songs as well as the popular troubadour songs and poetry. Like William of St. Thierry, they sought to "taste" divine love.

The beguines' love for those they served was in a sense the same love with which God loved humanity. This circulation of love flowed from the Beloved to humanity, a stream mingling in the ocean, light in which the duality of self and other, God and soul could be radically diminished. Through their practices they became, as Teresa of Avila would say a few centuries later, the hands and feet making God's love present in the world.

The Bramble and the Rose: Competing Visions of Christian Community

The beguine way of life produced a great flowering of spirituality in which women and men shared their insights and deepened their understanding of divine love. But this way of life was a stark challenge to an increasingly authoritarian church, which used both violence and ideology to make sure that religious symbols reinforced its authority. Official theology portrayed the anger of God punishing humanity with never-ending fire. Christ stepped in to take this condemnation on himself. Mercy depended on obedient participation in the church's penitential system. The clergy's possession of the keys to heaven or hell was a powerful instrument of political control, mediated by a strictly ordered hierarchy: the pope demanded obedience even of kings and bishops, priests obeyed their bishops, and laypeople obeyed priests; serfs obeyed masters, and women obeyed fathers and husbands. Violation of this order or the theology that undergirded it challenged the authority, power, and wealth of the religious and secular leaders. Even if it was not actively dissenting, an emphasis on free-flowing love, the unity of the Trinity in its love for humanity, and the opening of the mind in prayer outside the clerically supervised sacraments all seemed somewhat suspicious.

The poverty and simplicity of beguines and other contemplatives embodied an alternative to the wealth of the church. Their devotion to divine Lady Love contrasted a wrathful sovereign with a feminine image of gracious love. It is not that the beguines rejected the church and its sacraments, but their theology attested to a different understanding of who God is. Their very existence threw into question the exclusive authority of male clerics to determine Christian thought and practice. The mixture of rich and poor, clergy and laity, literate and illiterate in beguine communities challenged the rigid structuring of society. Their status as neither married laywomen nor enclosed nuns blurred the clear alternatives that defined true womanhood.

The Logic of Persecution

To some contemporary people, it may seem counterintuitive that women dedicated to service, prayer, and study would represent a threat to society. But listening to the way some religious leaders perceived these independent women uncovers the logic of persecution. William of St. Amour condemned beguines because they lacked formal supervision by clerics and were therefore a "breeding ground for moral turpitude and anticlericalism."[11] As defiance of their proper roles, laywomen's commitment to prayer, chastity, and poverty was a kind of immorality. It contrasted with clerics who were often vilified for their sexual indiscretions and luxurious living. Archbishops and popes placed their sons or (male) lovers in positions of influence and authority. This is not to say that all clerics were corrupt or that beguines never misbehaved, but this accusation against the beguines emphasizes the risk of unsupervised women and deflects from criticism of the clergy.[12]

For Franciscan friar Gilbert of Tournai, the possibility of thinking women was perhaps even more disturbing than their alleged moral turpitude:

> There are among us women called beguines some of whom blossom forth in subtleties and rejoice in novelties. They have interpreted in ordinary French idiom the mysteries of scripture that are accessible to experts in divine writing. They read them in common, irreverently, boldly, in conventicles, convents, and on squares. I have seen, read, and possessed the French bible, a copy of which has been displayed by the booksellers at Paris to record the heresies and errors, doubts and incorrect interpretations contained within them.[13]

We discover here that beguines had access to translations of the Bible available in Paris bookstalls. They apparently felt comfortable enough discussing theology and interpreting Scripture that they do so not only behind the high walls of convents but in informal study groups and even in public. From Gilbert's point of view, the Latin Vulgate is the only legitimate Bible precisely because translations would open it to the "unworthy." Scripture and theology are messy. If interpretation is open to the masses of laypersons, then variations are inevitable. This is disturbingly evident in the use of Scripture to justify apostolic poverty. The uneducated may imagine that Jesus' commissioning of Mary Magdalene as his messenger to the apostles justifies women's preaching. Thinking women are dangerous and immoral.

The End of an Era

Since the problem was that women were too independent, the obvious solution was to regulate them. Women closely supervised by vows, rules, and enclosure cannot violate standards for feminine behavior. Over the course of the thirteenth century, informal communities were replaced by walled beguinages that restricted women's movements. Access to the flow of conversation was more limited. "Good" (enclosed) beguines were distinguished from "bad" (unenclosed) beguines. Those carrying out the original vision of service in the community became almost by definition "bad" beguines. Even the plain clothing and veils beguines wore appeared to be symptoms of creeping heresy.

Presumably not by coincidence, beguine theology did not emerge from these convent-like beguinages but from the pens of unenclosed *magistras.*

Hadewijch of Brabant flourished in the beginning of the thirteenth century as a spiritual leader of a beguine community. But by the end of her life she was forced out of this role and separated from her community. During this same period, a German bishop threatened to excommunicate beguines who did not give up their habit. This may be the reason Mechthild of Magdeburg spent the final years of her life in a Cistercian convent. After Marguerite Porete's execution in 1310, the Council of Vienne of 1311–12 associated beguines with heresy and condemned their way of life.[14] Enclosed women continued lives of prayer and poverty, but the flowering of beguine theology came to an abrupt end.

But history is complex. The movement itself was crippled by persecution, but its writings survived. After her execution, Marguerite's book circulated anonymously and in many languages throughout Europe. The first translator of Marguerite's *Mirror* into modern English knew her only as "anonymous." "In a supreme irony, he concluded that, because the book was so finely argued, it must have been written by one of the theologians of the University of Paris—the very group which had condemned Marguerite to death."[15] The influence of Marguerite, Mechthild, and Hadewijch can also be seen in theologians such as Meister Eckhart and John Ruysbroek and through them, they continue to inspire Christian contemplative theology.

Women found other forms of life to explore their distinctive wisdom: third order Franciscans or Dominicans or semi-independent monasteries. Julian was not a beguine but an anchoress. Symbolically dead to the world, she was one of the last great women theologians of the Middle Ages. "Many waters cannot quench love" (Song 8:7). The writings of these great theologians have survived, a hush arbor of divine love secreted in the by-ways of history. "Marguerite calls the liberated soul a 'phoenix,' a characterization that could apply equally well to the author of the *Mirror of Simple Souls*" and to women's theology itself.[16] The next three chapters will introduce the story of each of these women.

2

I Must Give My Bride, Holy Christianity, a New Cloak

Mechthild of Magdeburg (1210–1282/94)

For when the cloak is old,
So is it cold.
And so I must give my bride, Holy Christianity, a new cloak.[1]

"Reformed and always reforming" is a motto of those denominations that were born from the traumas that cleaved Christianity in Western Europe into Catholic and Protestant branches. Over two hundred years earlier, Mechthild seemed to understand her own writing as part of an ongoing renewal of the church, the always fresh story of divine love for the world. She was discouraged by much of what she saw, and she hoped for a better day. But during her lifetime she was a vigorous voice of protest and hope.

Mechthild in Magdeburg

Little is known about Mechthild, though her name indicates that she lived most of her life in Magdeburg, near the border between German-speaking and Slavic territory. Though she chose a life of loneliness and poverty, her ability to read and write and her familiarity with the poetry of courtly love indicate that she was from a reasonably affluent family. A pious child, she was twelve when her almost daily "greetings" by the Holy Spirit began. As a young woman of about twenty she moved to Magdeburg, a city where she knew only one person, perhaps a Dominican friar. She lived as a beguine for most of the rest of her life. Though she mentions other beguines and it is speculated that she was their teacher, it is unclear what kind of community she lived in.

In her forties, she was persuaded by her confessor to begin writing down her visions and insights, which she continued to do for several decades. The last section of her book is written from a Cistercian convent in which, old and nearly blind, she was cared for by the sisters. The year of her death is disputed. Beyond inferences from her book, little else can be gleaned of her long life.

Mechthild's Book

Mechthild's beautiful and bold book *The Flowing Light of the Godhead* is among the first religious writings in Middle Low German. By writing in her native language, she makes her spiritual journey and her theological reflections available to women and laypeople. Her writing is intense and vivid, filled with metaphors, poetry, extended visual allegories, sighs, ecstasies, advice, and theological reflections.

Because writing and publishing is so commonplace in our own time, it may be difficult to imagine how radical and courageous an act it was for Mechthild to pick up her pen. It is easy to count the writings known to be written by women in Germany in the Middle Ages. Religious writing was an activity of educated clerics. Theology was the work of ordained men. Spiritual writing was done by celibate men and very occasionally by nuns such as Hildegard of Bingen. In writing a book, Mechthild was entering precarious territory.

She justifies writing her book because she was compelled by her confessor, who believed that her writing was divine revelation. One scribe copying out her book affirms that it had "flowed out of the living Godhead into Sister Mechthild's heart" and was faithfully set down by her own hand just as it was given to her.[2] From the point of view of this enthusiastic admirer, we understand that she was essentially taking dictation. After her death, Dominican friars appended descriptions of Mechthild's great holiness and affirmed that book was the work of the Holy Trinity revealed to a holy woman.[3]

Inspiration and Social Criticism

But these affirmations of her book's revelatory quality may not fully explain her motivation or do credit to the originality of her theological voice. We can glean from her "apostolic" way of life and her frequent criticisms of clergy that she was disillusioned by the corruption of the church's leadership. She seems compelled to write not only because a confessor is impressed by her interesting visions but also because she is passionately committed to the Dominican mission of reforming the church. Her theology, like all theology, is not merely personal or even spiritual, but fundamentally social and even political.

Her disgust with the church's leadership is evident throughout her book. At one point, she envisions Christ as a pilgrim who had been "trudging through all of Christendom." When asked where he was coming from, he answered: "'I'm coming from Jerusalem.' By that he meant Christianity. 'I have been driven from my shelter. The heathens do not acknowledge me, the Jews do not want me, Christians attack me.'"[4] Christians want no more to do with Jesus than non-Christians.

She traces this betrayal all the way to the top. She envisions this pilgrim Jesus lambasting the pope with excoriating criticism:

> Woe, Crown of Holy Christianity, how greatly have you been defiled. Your precious stones have slipped from you, for you sicken and ravage the holy Christian faith; your gold is deteriorated into a pool of impurity, for you are impoverished and have no love; your purity is obstructed by your lustful, firey piggishness; your humility is sunk in the swamp of your flesh. . . .O crown of holy priesthood, how you have sunk! . . . Those who do not know the way to hell, look to the corrupt priests, how their lives go straight to hell with wives and with children and other exposed sins.[5]

Mechthild envisioned purifying rather than breaking with the church, but her language foreshadows Luther's strident condemnation of its "Babylonian captivity."

By contrast, she writes devotedly of Dominic and his order.[6] Their austerity and their dedication to pastoral care for poor and laypeople provided an alternative vision of true Christianity. In this same vision, Christ indicates that the church requires a "new coat," that is, the renewing fervor of the Dominicans.

> "When the cloak is old,
> so is it cold.
> So I must bring to my bride, holy Christianity, a new cloak.'"[7]

Mechthild, of course, was excluded from preaching, but her book was a way to contribute to this promise of real renewal. The existence of her book is a sign of how important this mission was to her. Criticizing the church could be risky business, even in this period before the inquisition was in full swing. Writing as a woman violated the cultural space allotted her. She seems to have believed that what she had to say was critically important to the process by which the church would be called back to its original mission. She had been granted visions and insights not for her private amusement but in order to share them with the church during its time of dire need. This sense of urgency and mission compelled her to overcome the many barriers to writing.

A Burning Book?

Mechthild continued to write for several decades, until very near her death. Over the course of those years her fresh and beautiful poetry gave way to complex theological proposals. Trenchant criticisms take the form of visions of erring clerics in purgatory. She describes anguish over conflict with "Pharisees," that is, clerics or Dominicans who attacked her. She does not appreciate the vulnerability to which her writing exposed her. She upbraids her divine lover for imposing the task of writing on her, only to leave her threatened and afraid.

> I was warned against writing this book and people said: "if one was not careful, it would be burned on the fire." As when I was a child, I turned to pray: "Now I am distressed for your honor. If you do not comfort me now, you will have misled me, because you told me to write it yourself." Holding the book in his right hand, the lord said: "My love, do not be troubled. No one can burn the truth. Whoever took it from my hand would have to be stronger than me."[8]

Mechthild reports this scene fairly early in her text which suggests that though some friars admired her, she was also threatened, frightened, and harassed. Mechthild was caught up in the hazardous riptides of thirteenth century religious politics. Like her beloved Dominicans, she wanted to contribute to the purification of the church. But they were not uniform in their appreciation of her help.

Some Dominicans embraced the work of beguines and other holy women, recognizing their shared devotion. It was through the Dominicans that her work came into existence, was translated into other languages, and circulated. At the same time, the reforming zeal of the Dominicans was quickly appropriated by the pope, who used them as "hounds of God," hunting down heretics. Dominic began his work as a way to convert Albigensians back to orthodoxy, hoping the friars' discipline, holiness, and persuasive arguments would inspire dissenters. But over the course of the thirteenth century, the Dominicans also became the primary instruments of the inquisition. In part through their work, its machinery of interrogation was greatly refined. Paradoxically, zealous commitment to evangelical poverty or criticism of ecclesial wealth and ambition could be signs of "heresy."

In this context, it was easy to fall on the wrong side of the law. The practice of executing people for heretical ideas was not yet common, though it was on its way. Mechthild was in the position of being compelled by her confessor to write down profound and inspired religious poetry, social criticism, and theology. At the same time, as a laywoman criticizing the laxity of the clergy and offering a vision of divine love, it was easy for her to come into conflict with those who found her work threatening.

These transitions are captured in a vision Mechthild reports late in life. When she is surprised to see a Dominican she had known in purgatory, he explains that ostensibly holy people had turned him against innocent people and because of this he is made to suffer in purgatory. Mechthild mildly observes that it was because he listened to liars that his good intentions were perverted, and he was forced to suffer in purgatory.[9]

This vision captures the dangerous waters in which religious people swam. If they listened to their leaders, they were likely to see heresy where it did not exist. They may harass or condemn innocent people and end up paying the penalty for their mistake in an afterlife. If they did not, they may fall under suspicion themselves.

A Convent, "Sweet Hope," and Legacy

By the end of Mechthild's life, we find her enclosed in a Cistercian convent in Helfta. Church officials were beginning to insist that beguines stop wearing their distinctive habit or even choose between the convent or marriage. She may have been forced into a convent because she was a beguine or because she was outspoken.

There is also indication that by her sixties she was ill and mostly blind. Her last writings were dictated to sisters in the convent. Whether she went willingly or not, the convent provided her with needed care and a community in which she, old, sick, and blind, was able to continue her work of inspiration and renewal. She prays with gratitude that others must feed her, see for her, and use their hands for her. She prays that in all that is done and undone, in all that she suffers, that "your praise will never grow silent in my heart."[10]

Mechthild writes sympathetically about the struggles the nuns experience, including their own conflicts with clerical authority. But she also writes as someone who is not happy to be where she is. She seems to be a little awed by the superior education of the nuns and frustrated by the waning of her spiritual intensity. Her Beloved comforts her, saying that in her youth they were lovers but as an old woman she is his *haus-frau*—his (virgin) wife.

Her last entry is written not long before her death. She describes loneliness and suffering as her nuptial garments, preparing her for her final union with her Beloved. She reconciles even with her body, so often reviled by her for the way it distracted her from contemplation: "Oh, my very dear prison, in you I have been bound, I thank you for everything, that you have followed me; alone I distressed you, but you still came to my help." She concludes with confidence that all will soon be well as she continues to "hold firmly onto sweet hope."[11]

After her death, the nuns remembered her kindly and even had visions of her in heaven. Mechthild may have been unhappy at finding herself enclosed in a convent. But Gertrude the Great and Mechthild of Hackeborn were both inspired by her example to write. Both in her own work and in her inspiration of others, she contributed to the flowering of women's spiritual writings.

Mechthild's original book was modified and translated into Latin and another German dialect after her death. A copy was sent to at least one community of Benedictine nuns. The book was known to the famous Dominican theologian Meister Eckhart, whose writings were influenced by it.[12] But after that it seems to disappear until it was rediscovered in 1861.

The Tides of History

Mechthild's life encompasses the changing attitudes toward the beguines. As a young and middle-aged woman she appears to be respected and well regarded. She is encouraged to enter her vocation, possibly by a Dominican friar. She lived several decades among friars and beguines, experimenting with ascetical practices, dedicated to a life of prayer and contemplation, and contributing to a theology that was congenial to the aspirations of women and men devoted to spiritual practice and ecclesial renewal. By the end of her life, she was secreted away in a convent; she was out of circulation and no longer participating in the public conversations that were available to unenclosed beguines. The church seemed successful in silencing her hymn to Lady Love, even without resorting to violence.

3

Obey No Created Thing except Love

Marguerite Porete (Died 1310)

"Lady Love: Charity does not obey any created thing except love."[1]

Marguerite Porete is certainly the boldest, in her writing and in her life, of the beguines. She was a martyr to the truth of divine love and the perhaps more disturbing truth that women can teach something about this love. I admit that Marguerite evokes my deepest admiration. As a theologian, I have rarely read anyone for whom the *via negativa* and a theology of divine love are so profoundly interwoven.[2] As a feminist wounded by the patriarchal structures of the church and its often harsh theology, I feel indebted to her enormous courage. Out of her deep wells of compassion, she was able to remain unbowed when church authorities burned first her book and then her body.

As someone who teaches theology and tries to inspire others, not least women, to study, teach, and preach, I am pained that my work would have been a capital offense in previous centuries. It does not seem natural to me that the church would savagely murder a woman for writing theology any more than it is natural that it would provide a theology to underwrite American slavery. The scar of that is not entirely healed: many of my women graduate students struggle against internal voices that condemn their work; many women feel marginalized or driven away from church leadership. As one pastor wrote to me:

> I am also teary reading about Marguerite's life. Tears means it connected, but I think as a clergy woman that was easier for me than for less involved men or women that can ignore the internalized sexism of the church as an institution, and who have not been subjected to the daily slights of its members. I have lost my closest colleagues in

> ministry to men who abused their power and supervisors who hurt them, sometimes undermining them physically but mostly harming them spiritually by questioning their devotion to the church as they tried to be mother, breadwinner, and pastor.

The church is impoverished by the destruction of this great theologian—and by the loss of all women who are defrauded of their vocation. I feel that we owe a debt to her to carry on the work of theology written by women and, through us, by and for the church and the world. Perhaps in your life and in your teaching and preaching, dear readers, the church will continue its healing from this wounding loss.

A "Beguine Clergeresse"

Marguerite, called "the Porete," lived in the French-speaking province of Hainault, on the border between Belgium and France. It was a place of enormous religious vitality. On both sides of the river thousands of beguines congregated in the many large and small beguinages spread throughout the area.

We can imagine them as a community engaged in frequent debate with one another, discussing meditation and theology and perhaps even translating the Scriptures into the vernacular.[3] They would often gather around someone whose spiritual practice and wisdom granted her the authority of a *magistra*, that is, a female teacher.[4] We may infer that Marguerite was such a *magistra*, a master of contemplative practices and theological reflection who was dedicated to her teaching vocation. In some copies of her manuscript she is referred to by the unusual honorific, "beguine clergeresse," that is, a clerical beguine. This term suggests that her writing style is more like that of the educated clergy and that, for some, it possessed authority normally restricted to them.[5]

But in contrast to many traditional clerical writings, she offers a gentler style of practice, a theology of love rather than wrath, and a deep respect for women. Beyond the constraints of reason, will, and desire, and beyond the teachings of a misogynistic church hierarchy, there remains a joyful peace that the world can neither give nor take away. Although her book is difficult, she is important to contemporary seekers, ministers, and students because of her confidence in a love that knows no bounds and her evocation of nondualistic awareness.[6] She witnesses to the beautiful luminosity in the human soul and the joy that arises as we reconnect to its divine source.

"I Certainly Cannot Be Silent in order to Save the Whole Word"[7]

That Marguerite's book exists at all is somewhat astonishing. Thinking about her determination to write may help interpret her theology. As we saw with

Mechthild, women's writing was unusual. It was also expensive. She would have to raise considerable sums for the materials to produce even one or two versions of her text. Since it appears that there were several copies in circulation during her lifetime, we must imagine a great deal of time and money dedicated to copying out the hundred and fifty pages of her book on vellum by hand. This points to a community willing to expend its time and resources to circulate her writings.

We do not have access to her interior life, but there are clues in her text that may account for her dedication to keep her book in circulation. Marguerite writes quite poignantly about the need for a book such as hers. "But I wanted to speak of him because no one would tell me . . . and Lady Love told me the truth; it is this which soothes me."[8] She herself longed for a teacher. She crashed against the limitations of what she was taught, her heart yearning for more. But no one was there to teach her. Though she understands the limits of trying to tell of the greatness of divine goodness, hearing Love's teachings and sharing them with others is the only thing that comforts her.[9] The urgency of her writing arises from the need to witness to others, not only the depth of divine mystery and love but also to indicate that the theology available to her fellow beguines is misleading and harmful.

Instead of the stream of rhetoric describing women as inferior, sinful, morally weak, intellectually useless, incapable of either understanding or self-control, she sets out a dialogue among three feminine personifications (Lady Love, the Soul, and Reason). Instead of the harsh and austere God, enthroned like a human emperor or pope, Lady Love leads her into the divine abyss beyond images. Reason implores her: "Ah, Lady Love, for the mercy of God, tell it to us, not only for those nourished on my crumbs, but for those who have taken leave and me and will be, if God pleases, illuminated by this book."[10] A feminine Reason implores Love to teach those contemplatives who remain bound by discursive reason and by the more narrow teachings of the church.[11]

What Marguerite teaches is advanced but not at odds with other contemplative theologians. The primacy of divine love is the center of the contemplative path, evident in Marguerite's near contemporaries: Thomas Aquinas, William of St Thierry, or Beatrice of Nazareth. But she is an unenclosed woman teaching this to other unsupervised women. She is drawing the conclusions that if God is love, harsh or self-abnegating penances may do more harm than good. She is also drawing the conclusion that there is a spiritual sphere that is not under the control of discursive reason and, by implication, the scholarly men who police Christian thought.

It may be that many modern people find themselves in a situation much like that of these hungry and thirsty beguines. One's heart may have some deep intuition of an abyss of divine love, a wonder and mystery so much sweeter, more spacious than the language of the liturgy. Familiar images of God may seem banal or limiting. One might feel lost and alone and find no one to teach how to move from a child's faith to one of a mature adult. It is easy to find oneself in an arid place, unable to move forward or backward. To doubt is to be without spiritual nurture. To stay is to let some part of oneself die.

Through her book Marguerite is encouraging contemplatives not only to believe but also experience that God is love; this awareness is what transforms the heart and makes abiding peace possible. It was dangerous for Marguerite to write her book; in the end it cost her life. But she did not want others to feel the same loneliness and confusion that tormented her. "Lady Love told her the truth" and this truth was not for Marguerite alone. It was food and drink for all of the hungry and thirsty ones, aching for news of the divine Beloved.

A "False Woman"

The story of Marguerite's fate is complicated but will be told here as simply as possible.[12] Sometime between 1296 and 1306, Marguerite's book was burned in her presence by her local bishop, the Bishop of Cambrai, in Valenciennes (now France), which would now be about a forty-five minute drive by car from her native Hainaut (now Belgium). When that bishop died, she sought to have the condemnation overturned by the new bishop. She attempted to do this by adding a different conclusion and gaining the approval of three highly esteemed religious authorities: a Franciscan friar, Brother John; a Cistercian monk, Dom Franco of the abbey at Villiers; and most significantly, Master of Theology Godfrey of Fontaines, a doctor of the University of Paris and thus one of the authoritative theologians of the day. These three were well chosen not only because of their spotless reputations but also because they represented three quite different spheres of authority: a friar, an enclosed monk, and a scholastic theologian. Apparently ignorant of the larger swirls of church politics in which she was becoming enmeshed, she seemed to think that if these three very different sources of authority approved her writing, it would be reconsidered by the new bishop. Instead, he had her arrested and handed over to King Philip the Fair's political ally, confessor, and chief inquisitor, William of Paris. She was held in his prison for eighteen months, during which time she refused to confess or otherwise cooperate with her accusers.

This silence has been variously interpreted. Looking at external events, it is plausible to infer that once she was arrested she realized her cause was lost. *The Mirror of Simple Souls* eerily foreshadows what a person in this position might do. In the dialogue with Reason, the frustrated Soul bemoans the necessity of silence before those who prefer death to the peace that comes from Love. Because of their rudimentary and hostile literalism, she will be compelled to keep "silence and conceal my language, which I learned . . . at the secret court of the sweet country, where courtesy is law, and love moderates, and we are nourished on goodness."[13] It is a little disquieting to consider that this was written before her text was condemned and yet so tellingly reflects her fate. In the face of executioners who demanded that she recant, there was nothing to do but remain silent.

After eighteen months, the theology faculty of Paris was called to deliberate at her trial, orchestrated by William of Paris. Fifteen sentences from her book were read, without regard to their meaning or context, and assessed to be heretical. She was condemned as a relapsed heretic and handed over to the secular arm. Soldiers took her to a field in Paris, where she was tied to a stake and burned alive. Marguerite was among the first women to be burned in Paris for heresy, helping to inaugurate one of the darkest periods of Christian history.

Why Marguerite?

I have read many scholars and many pages puzzling over why Marguerite was burned. Her theology was not markedly different from other beguines or Cistercians. The more provocative statements that were quoted, indicating that she no longer need be governed by virtue or reason, are qualified by the insistence that this freedom only arises when desire is so utterly aligned with the divine will that the desire to behave badly had been eradicated. "Virtues, I take leave of you forever and my heart is completely free and gay."[14] But this Soul is so free and gay because "all of her exterior desires and interior sentiments and all affections of the spirit are made nothing [*adnientiee*] so that whatever she does is according to the habit of good practice or by the commandment of Holy Church, without desire, because her will, which causes desire, is dead."[15] Because Reason continues to be disturbed by this, she explains again: such a Soul "neither desires nor despises poverty or tribulation, nor mass nor sermon, nor fast nor prayer and gives to Nature everything that is necessary without qualm of conscience; *but* this nature is so well ordered by transformation in unity with Love to which the will of this Soul is conjoined, that nature demands nothing that would be forbidden."[16] She views freedom as arising only when the spring of agency has been taken over by the divine will. Freedom can do more than external virtues require but not less.

In any case, since her book circulated unimpeded when it was anonymous or attributed to a man, it may have been her gender that was the real problem. According to her less sympathetic modern interpreters, she was executed because she was "stubborn," "intolerant of criticism," and "her proselytizing was inimical to [the Inquisition's] authority."[17] Put differently, she refused to acquiesce to silence and enclosure, and this was perceived to be incompatible with the concentration of ideological control in the hands of the Inquisition and the king it served. Many interpreters point out that because she was unenclosed and without an obvious male defender, she was vulnerable in a way that someone like Mechthild was not. Some interpreters infer from the number of texts in circulation during her lifetime, including at least one already translated into Latin before her death, that she was a popular and important teacher. "Given the strength of the persecution against her, she may have had a considerable following."[18]

She was a writer. This, too, was unusual, though it was the way she wrote that is likely to have been particularly noteworthy. She placed herself outside the pale of clerical protection by eschewing the strategies that protected someone like Mechthild. She did not appeal to penitential agonies or divine ecstasies. She did not hate her female body or torture it with penitential outrages. Her writing refuses the self-effacing rhetoric one finds in Mechthild, (the early) Julian, Teresa of Avila, and many others. These women lamented their inferiority in various ways, insisting: I am but a stupid woman; illiterate, I know nothing; far be it from me to be a teacher. By contrast, Marguerite did not veil her theological insights and social critique by putting them in the mouth of Christ.

She wrote "like a man." Her genre is a dialogue among personifications of Lady Love, Reason, and the Soul. It may be partly modeled after *The Romance of the Rose*. It is not unlike Boethius's *Consolation of Philosophy*, though it lacks (except retroactively) the dramatic context of his prison cell.[19] She engages in genuine theological reflection and does so with great sophistication. Her God has a feminine element who engages in conversation with an intelligent feminine soul. Both in her style of life and her style of writing, she violated the boundaries of true womanhood—a fact emphasized by the chronicler of her trial, William of Nangis, who dismisses her as a "false woman," (*pseudo-muliere*) as he describes her "hardened malice" and refusal to repent.

Why Marguerite? Perhaps her "unwomanly" behavior may explain why she was a good choice for Philip the Fair's performance of piety. With one fiery drama he proves his orthodoxy in the most succinct way: neither theological speculation nor brazen women will be tolerated by a God-fearing loyal son of the faith. The public spectacle of living flesh agonizingly transformed into flame seems calculated to put an end not to her thought, which continued to live, but to the appalling possibility that women would write or think or teach about religion.

In the immediate aftermath of her death, the Council of Vienne 1312, quoting passages from her text, brought an end to the theological creativity of the beguine movement.

Resurrection

Marguerite's book continued to circulate surprisingly widely. There were copies in Italy, France, the Lowlands, and England. It was translated into Latin and Middle English. It was admired by Marguerite Navarre and influenced Meister Eckhart. Her theology and insight were remarkable enough to be confused with a master of theology at the University of Paris, a Cistercian monk, and John Ruysbroeck. Scholars such as Amy Hollywood are restoring it to a place in Christian history and thought. That she was also a remarkable person is suggested by the courage and calm she evinced under the most terrifying circumstances.

It turns out that it was easier than Mechthild anticipated to "burn the truth." But, as Marguerite herself says, truth is phoenix-like. It continually reappears, wearing the guise appropriate to new historical moments. After Marguerite's death, women acquiesced to enclosure and silence. But in a tiny cell across the English Channel, Lady Love would find another devotee who would pen her own paean to the mystery of divine goodness: "a revelation of love that Jesus Christ, our endless bliss, made in sixteen showings" to a "simple, unlettered creature."[20]

4

I Saw No Wrath Anywhere

Julian of Norwich (Born 1342)

> "And in this beholding I thought it necessary to see that we are sinners and do many evils. . . . wherefore we deserve pain, blame, and wrath. And notwithstanding all of this, I saw most steadfastly that our lord was never wrathful nor ever shall be."[1]

Julian is perhaps the most familiar of our female trinity, but this should not disguise her greatness as a theologian. Grace Jantzen is among many who identify her as one whose literary skill ranks her "with Chaucer as a pioneering genius of English prose."[2] Thomas Merton describes her as one of the greatest Christian theologians.[3] T. S. Eliot quotes her affirmation that all will be well at the conclusion of "Little Gidding," as German bombs were raining down on England and even on Julian's church. Denise Levertov wrote a cycle of poems about her. Annie Dillard alludes to her in *Holy the Firm*. Rowan Williams characterizes her book as "what may well be the most important work of Christian reflection in the English language."[4] In addition to these poets, scholars, and fellow mystics, her legacy has produced a small industry in contemporary devotional texts and even blogs.

And yet this revered and beloved woman spent the last decades of her life in a ten by twelve foot cell. The consecration of an anchoress is performed by a bishop and includes rites for the dead. Entering into the anchor-hold is death to the world, a remembrance of death, and a commitment to remain there until death. She was separated from life by the ritual for the dying in her tiny anchor-hold, a symbolic tomb.

The Long but Obscure Life of Lady Julian

As with the other theologians we are studying, little can be definitively known about Julian. The first mystery is her name. She shares the name of the church to which she was attached later in life as an anchoress. Some scholars have inferred that she took the name of the church as her own when she entered her anchor-hold. Father John-Julian argues that not a single anchor-hold in this period lent its name to its inhabitant.[5] There are records of several women named Julian in Norwich, so it is likely that those who called her Lady Julian in her own time knew her real name.

Some argue that she had been a nun; some surmise she was married and had children. There is also no agreement whether she was illiterate or a polyglot in possession of a formidable scholastic education. Whatever her background, she wrote charming and sophisticated English prose and explored theological ideas with great subtlety.

What is known is that she was born in 1342 and some thirty years later, on May 13, 1372, she became extremely ill and appeared to be dying. Her mother was with her, and a cleric was called for to give her last rites; he held a cross up to console her. Instead of dying, she experienced a long and detailed set of visions ("showings") that began with vivid depictions of Christ's passion and went on to unfold the seeds of a dramatic retelling of the Christian story and its theological significance. She was enclosed in an anchor-hold sometime after 1373. At some point, possibly very soon after the event, she wrote a short version of her visions and at least twenty years later a much longer version that includes her mature theological reflections. Margery Kempe visited her around 1413. Wills record small amounts of money left to her and her servants in her anchor-hold until 1429. And then—silence.

Three Wounds

Julian is very precise about the events from which her theological reflections spring. On May 13 of 1373 when she was thirty and a half years old she became very ill. On the fourth night she was believed to be dying and received last rites. She lingered for another three days. A priest brought a crucifix to comfort her last moments. She fixed her eyes on the crucifix, expecting to die at any moment. The room became dark and filled with fiends; only the crucifix remained light. Suddenly all of her pain passed away. As she lay taking what she believed were her last breaths, her thoughts turned to a prayer for "three wounds" she had made years before but had subsequently forgotten.[6]

Her prayer was to participate in Christ's passion and in this way enter more deeply into Christ's compassion for humanity. Meditation on the passion was a familiar practice during the Middle Ages. By participating in Christ's pain, one would feel intense remorse for sin and gratitude for redemption. Her prayer was somewhat different. The "first wound" was to experience the compassion Mary Magdalene and the others would have felt at the cross. She would know, through a bodily sight, Jesus' suffering and his friends' anguish; this would allow her to "have the more true mind of the passion of Christ."[7] It is intriguing that she wished to know not only what Christ suffered but also what Mary and Mary Magdalene and all of his "lovers" felt. It was not only the gore of physical suffering and the guilt we should feel for provoking it she prayed for; she also wished to know the heart of compassion as it flowed through the tight-knit circle that adored Christ.

The second "wound" was to experience a mortal illness during which she would be so "hard on to death" she would receive last rites. She hoped in this way she would be purged by the mercy of God and live afterward in greater worship of God.[8] The first wound is an experience of the death of Christ and the suffering of his friends, the second wound would be an experience of her own mortality. Together, this visceral awareness of suffering, death, and compassion would enable her to take on the "mind of Christ."[9]

The third wound is itself three wounds: contrition, compassion, and longing for God. This prayer, trinitarian in form, represents the fundamental shape of her piety. Contrition is a recognition of the way sin separates us from God. Compassion is recognition of the nature of God, present in the entire Trinity and distinctively manifest in the passion. Longing for God is longing for intimacy with Christ. It is also the ability to hear and see the wounds of the world and to alleviate them by her witness to the radical goodness and love of God. Union with Christ's compassion for humanity would be the primary route to the joyousness of the divine presence. Even her early piety, which she had herself forgotten, was guided by the spirit of compassion.

As she lay apparently on the verge of death she remembered her prayer for a mortal illness and for a sight of Christ's passion. This is precisely what unfolded over many hours. Through visual sight, spiritual sight, and spiritual understanding she was introduced into a theology of divine love that was so complete and radical that it utterly bewildered her. When she woke up, she immediately renounced it as a delirium. This provided the pretext for the devil to appear to her, to hold her by the throat to silence and kill her. Jesus intervenes once more to assure her that she must believe in what she saw and hold on to it for her entire life.

Upon her recovery, she entered the anchor-hold at St. Julian's church and continued to meditate on what she had seen. She wrote an initial version of her "showings" sometime between 1382 and 1388 (often referred to as the Short Text). She remained dissatisfied with her understanding of what she had been shown and continued to struggle over its meaning for another twenty years. She received two additional inner teachings during this period that finally enabled her to write the much longer *A Revelation of Divine Love*, now widely regarded as one of the single most important theological documents in the English language.

Julian's Anchor-Hold

What does it mean to enter an anchor-hold? To the contemporary person, it seems a bizarre and cruel fate to be bricked into a cell without the possibility of ever leaving. But for many medieval women, this prisonlike structure could become a space of astonishing freedom.

The beguine movement had few adherents in England and anchor-holds provided an alternative to convents and marriage. There were in this period as many as fifteen or twenty anchoresses in or near Norwich.[10] Other women were attracted to the more overt criticism of the church afforded by the pre-Reformation "Lollard" movement. For Julian, rebellion against the church was not an option. Her vocation was within the institutional church, and her showings were given for the good of other Christians, not for her private benefit. She was in contact with various monks and nuns, who formed an informal network of conversation. Speaking to and within the church was important to her.

At the same time, the church was in a state of almost unthinkable chaos, both at the local and international levels. Her allegiance did not appear to be blind. In one of her rare allusions to the turmoil of her time she writes: "Holy church shall be shaken in sorrow and anguish and tribulation in this world as men shake a cloth in the wind. . . . For he says: 'I shall tear you away from your vain affections and your viscious pride. And after that I shall gather you together, and make you meek and mild, clean and holy, by one-ing you to myself.'"[11]

Whatever led her to her anchor-hold, it was a place of great intellectual freedom and security. In it, she could meditate without distraction on the showings that had been given to her. She could write and then rewrite a theology that interpreted the astonishing message she received. Enclosure and discipline seems to have been for her spaciousness and joy. Nonetheless, it was a radical decision.

An anchor-hold is a small cell, typically one or two rooms attached to a church. It is sealed from the outside but has a window opening onto the church sanctuary and a window opening onto the street. These windows are curtained so the anchoress remains invisible, but she is able to converse with people. She can provide spiritual council and receive spiritual conversation. There is a door onto a separate room where her servant lives and works.

Her cell would have included a simple bed, a desk, a chest, an altar, and various small items for study, washing, sewing, and so on. She would have been dressed more or less like a nun. Like everyone else, she drank beer. Her day would be structured by the divine office, which left many hours for her own study, meditation, and writing as well as time to meet with townspeople, to whom she was an important counselor and advisor.[12] Such a life is replete with austerities and yet, even with moderate fasting, her diet was better than that of a peasant or serf. Because her voice is so soothing, it is easy to imagine her in serene circumstances, ensconced in a smooth-running anchor-hold secure against ordinary human vicissitudes. But this calm is like a tiny raft riding out a tsunami of catastrophe.

Her theology is really a theodicy: it is a long and profound reflection on how Christians can possibly orient themselves to a world that has gone under. She is a teacher to us as we, too, face the prospect of environmental collapse, plague, bitter divides between wealth and poverty, atrocities we thought humanity had put behind it, and endless war. Her confidence in divine love is serene and strong, but we have to remember it is in the context of social disaster. Barbara Tuchman describes the fourteenth century as a "distant mirror" of our own time. Understanding the historical context of her theology may make it more compelling as we face our own tragedies.

"Under the Broad Water"

"One time my understanding was led down into the sea ground, and there I saw green hills and dales. Then I understood thus: that if a man or woman were there, under the broad water, and he have a sight of God—as God is with man continually—he would be safe in soul and body and take no harm."[13] This image dramatically captures the despair of being caught helplessly in flood tides and carried down to the bottom of the water to be drowned—but even here, we "take no harm." This is a main theme of her theology: no matter what our experience, even if we are sucked under the broad water of death and destruction, our confidence in divine love need never erode. This is not only a poetic image. In 1362 a terrible flood washed over Norwich, washing away farms and families. Storm surges reached thirty feet, and parts of Norwich were under fifteen feet of water. Twenty thousand cattle and thirty thousand sheep were lost.[14] Those who remember Hurricane Katrina or Sandy will recognize why this indelible memory would serve as a metaphor of devastating catastrophe. But this a relatively minor (!) disaster compared to the devastations that afflicted Julian and the people of Norwich.

Julian lived during the beginnings of the "Little Ice Age," when warm summers became less certain and heavy rains more so. Natural disasters in the form of climate change, famine, flood, and plague swept over Norwich in repeating waves. War, revolt, and brigandage matched natural disaster with a merciless epidemic of violence. The church's devotion to wealth and power entangled it in a cycle of disintegration, epitomized by the Great Schism. With two popes vying for authority, war and politically motivated crusades became the normal order. The political, ecclesial, and ideological structures of medieval feudalism were careening toward the violent changes that brought to birth the modern world.

The Black Death

In 1348 the first wave of the Black Death hit England. Norwich, located by the sea—with accompanying ships and rats—lost upwards of six out of ten of its populace. The plague killed swiftly and gruesomely. Dying children were abandoned by parents, wives by husbands. Though carts rolled through town collecting corpses to toss into mass graves, many human and animal bodies simply rotted where they fell. The sights, sounds, and smells would have been overwhelming. The fear that one could die at any moment would produce mind-numbing anxiety. The loss of friends and family affected everyone. Whole neighborhoods were left as ghost towns.

Clergy died along with everyone else, often giving last rites to the dying. The waves of Black Death created two thousand ecclesial vacancies in the area around Norwich alone. Without clergy, priests were not available for crucial tasks such as baptism, marriage, and last rites. People went to their doom unshriven, condemned to the fate of those who died in mortal sin. In the face of this religious catastrophe, bishops and popes allowed any recent confession to count, even one to a layperson or woman. Young men were brought into the priesthood who were uneducated and lacked any serious vocation. This low-ebb of leadership did little to shore up respect for the church.

After the first wave of the "pestilence" crested, there were few workers to plant or bring in crops and few clergy to tend to a population wholly dependent on the church for salvation. And yet this cycle repeated itself several times during Julian's life, making life feel terrifyingly precarious.[15]

War and Revolt

Natural disasters were underscored by human-caused ones. The Hundred Years' War between France and England roiled on, cresting in the years between outbreaks of the plague in 1340, 1346, 1356. The war was renewed by Henry V in 1415 and, having begun a few years before her birth, continued on for decades after Julian's death. Shelly Rambo has pointed out that Julian's anchor-hold was near the main street where maimed, sick, and demoralized soldiers found port upon their return. She argues that this proximity to war and its consequences informs Julian's own counterimages of peace and reconciliation.[16]

War produced veterans, some traumatized, some brutalized, many well-equipped psychologically to continue the violence that served them in warfare. The ravages of these returned soldiers could be as terrifying as natural disasters. Soldiers, freed from the stain of sin and its eternal consequences, turned to looting, brigandage, and other outrageous behaviors.

"And All Manner of Things Shall Be Well"

I have lingered so long over this litany of disasters because I believe it is essential to understanding Julian's theology. Any one of these things would be individually and collectively traumatizing: plague, warfare, a church in turmoil, natural disaster, political violence. Neither individuals nor societies survive these blows intact. Religious ideology matched the violence of the times. This is why theological criticism was understood (in a sense, correctly) as treason. The ideas that justify a system are as important as its soldiers and executioners.

The Black Death naturally made people turn to religion for an explanation. But in looking for answers, people tended to project that disaster onto a divine sovereign who was apparently enraged with them. Some unimaginably black and terrible sin must have provoked such a gruesome punishment. Only the most ferocious and terrifying deity would unleash the hideous death that assaulted everyone indiscriminately.

The vision that Julian received came to her just after the third cresting of the plague, the Great Famine, and the Great Flood. It was such a radical alternative to the teachings she knew that she was more dismayed than consoled. She watched from her window as the church writhed in self-created anguish, but she could not yet understand how her revelation connected to the theology of wrath that came in through her windows like rank air.

But the words that would shape her thinking are already recorded in the Short Text: "I will make all things well, I shall make all things well, I may make all things well and I can make all things well; and you shall see it yourself that all things will be well."[17] Though pain distracts us so that we no longer recognize God's love, this does not mean God has ceased loving us. We can completely trust this love, however great our pain. "For it is his will that we know that all the might of our enemy [the devil] is locked in our friend's [God's] hand."[18]

For some fifteen years she remained bewildered by what she had been shown. How could there be sin if God is sovereign? How could the radical love of her vision be reconciled with the church's teachings? Why was she shown neither wrath nor hell? "And fifteen years and more later, I was answered in spiritual understanding: 'What, would you know the lord's meaning in this thing? Know it well, love was his meaning. Who showed it to you? Love. What did he show you? Love. Why did he show it to you? For love. Hold this within, you shall know more of the same. But you will never know other than this without end.'"[19]

Julian tried to understand the goodness of God against the backdrop of astonishing suffering and dissolution. She tried to understand the undiluted goodness of God while respecting theological systems that justified the chaos and savagery that stalked every road and byway. We can understand her refrains "All will be well and all manner of things will be well," and "love was my meaning," and "I saw no wrath anywhere" only if we place them in the context of the heartrending suffering she witnessed throughout her life. Untangling the wisdom of her showings from the bellicose theology available to her was a long and difficult road. But as her understanding of her vision ripened into maturity, its full implications began to shine through.

We know nothing about the time or manner of Julian's death. Notwithstanding her local popularity as a spiritual guide, her text seemed to disappear, only to be uncovered centuries later.

PART 2

Lady Love and Mother Christ: Three Women's Spirituality of Compassion

5

"Her God-Hunting Heart"

Theology and the Spirituality of Desire

> Whenever the soul pursues love and the great hunger of her God-hunting heart has ascended the high mountain of profound love and beautiful knowledge, she acts like the pilgrim. . . .[1]

This brief historical background describes an arc from the early flourishing of contemplative women's writings to their repression and diminishment. But when we turn to the writings themselves, we are not left with death and burial: we experience resurrection as we immerse ourselves in a theological world that is governed by desire and the possibility of joy.

Though modern people may not realize it, desire was a key theme in Christian theology and contemplation for much of its history. The fourth century theologian, Gregory of Nyssa, collages biblical imagery to evoke God's desire for humanity. For Gregory, desire is the "wound" received by the bride in the Song of Songs. This "wound" opens the heart to union between the soul and God. The "Bowman" who wounded her is Love. Scriptures teach that God is love and that Christ is his "chosen arrow (Isa. 49.2)" with which he "unites to the Bowman whomsoever it strikes." "Indeed it is a good wound and a sweet pain by which life penetrates the soul; for by the tearing of the arrow she opens, as it were, a door, an entrance into herself. For no sooner does she receive the dart of love than the image of archery is transformed into a scene of nuptial joy."[2] Here Love is God, God's messenger, and the wound that draws God's beloved back into union. Love is the desire born in humanity for her Beloved. Desire circulates between lover and beloved and erodes the duality that separates them.

In the fifth century, Pseudo-Dionysius continues this emphasis on the divine Eros as the energy that creates the cosmos and restores the soul to its original lucidity. Religious desire is not an extrinsic emotion. It is not like wishing for something external to oneself—food, pleasure, security. It is a heart-energy that transforms the substance of humanity back into the divine image. Longing is not only *for* God; in a sense, it *is* God. It is through love that we abide in God and God in us (John 15). Speaking of God's lovers, Pseudo-Dionysius says, "their longing for the Good makes them what they are and confers on them their well-being. Shaped by what they yearn for, they exemplify goodness."[3] For Pseudo-Dionysius, as for Gregory, desire is not entirely self-generated. Humanity desires God because God desires humanity. Desire flows between us and unites us as water is poured into water. Human desire flows from divine desire: "The divine longing is Good seeking good for the sake of the Good. That yearning which creates all the goodness of the world preexisted superabundantly within the Good and did not allow it to remain without issue."[4]

Modern Christianity has tended to focus more on belief than desire. Fundamentalism is the extreme example of this: salvation depends on *believing* certain things. Unfortunately, too often this emphasis on belief fails to translate into a loving heart. But for theologians such as Gregory or Pseudo-Dionysius, it is the heart that matters. Belief and praise are ways to orient the heart toward the divine, but beliefs cannot themselves transform us into the divine goodness. Their theology is an attempt to find words for the awakening of the heart by love.

For readers who might have studied someone like Karl Barth and been indoctrinated in the absolute otherness of God, this delirium of delight may sound off-putting. Readers who have become familiar with Buddhist philosophy may find the anthropomorphic description of divine desire equally strange. It is a mistake to over-literalize these images. These theologians of desire had a clear sense of how religious language about God and the soul works. Images cannot touch the reality of divinity. Even the word "God" is too literal, especially if it brings to mind a mighty person in the sky. Like theologians before them, these women multiplied images and concepts to help us avoid clinging to any one: far/near, lover, mother, lord, empress, father, abyss, lady, Trinity. But working with the metaphor of desire was a way to describe and ignite the ferocity of the soul as it hungered for its ultimate truth, its source, its beyond-being goodness, its beyond-thought Beloved. In describing God as "desiring" humanity, they are poeticizing ultimate reality as undiluted good. The poetry of desire insists that to connect with this imageless ultimate reality is the sweetest of lives and the worthiest of deaths.

As we turn to the writings of Mechthild, Marguerite, and Julian, we will encounter forms of this ancient contemplative theology. We will see how desire pierces the soul, an "arrow" that opens the heart to intimacy with divine Love.

Mechthild's Burning Heart

Mechthild's erotic imagery captures the intensity of a desiring heart, willing to abandon everything for the Beloved. This desire becomes for her a pathway to transformation as well as a window into the nature of divine goodness and power. Through desire, she is linked to divine reality, transformed by it, and ready to witness to the profound love that arises from this intimate relationship. Hers is a wonderful testimony to the power of desire as a thread that joins us to the divine.

Lady Love: Empress and Eagle

Not long before her death, Mechthild described a complex tableau representing the centrality of divine Love. She pictures a procession of virgins led by a man resembling a love-lit bishop. Together, virgins and bishop serve a noble queen. Overhead, a radiant maiden in the form of a golden eagle oversees and arranges everything. The virgins personify the virtues while the man luminous with love signifies Christian faith. Through faith and virtue, humanity serves its queen: Lady Love. But it is this feminine eagle representing the full power of divine Love that oversees the scene. It is Love that animates virtue and faith. It is Love that illuminates and orders both divinity and humanity. "This love dwells in Christian faith; she rests in the palace of her lady, the queen. It is her office to pull love to love, God to the soul, and the soul to God. That is why she is placed as the first commandment."[5] In this image, Love enables us to love and serve God. Love makes us human and God, God. Love is who we are and it is also what connects Lady Love (God) to humanity and humanity to God.

"When Two Desire Together, There Love Is Complete:"[6]

The love that is the subject and object of faith is an almost erotic love that flows between God and humanity. Our love for God is possible only because God first loves us. This love is an intense divine longing that is the foundation of all of God's actions in creation and redemption.

In Mechthild's poetry, divine Love sings to the Soul as a lover might speak to his beloved:

O you beautiful rose in the thorns!
O you fluttering bee in the honey!
O you pure dove in your nature!
O you beautiful sun in your shining!
O you full moon in your standing!
I cannot turn away from you.[7]

We may experience the predations of sin, the sufferings of the human body, and the limitations of the Soul's capacities. But our divine lover sees the Soul's truest self, the great luminosity with which she is created. God delights in this beauty. It is the Soul's birthright that remains unstained by sin and is resuscitated by redemptive love. The intimacy between the Soul and God is expressed in the longing and satisfaction of God.

You are my softest pillow,
My most lovely bed,
My most intimate rest,
My deepest longing,
My highest honor.
You are a desire of my Godhead,
A thirst for my humanity,
A stream for my passion.[8]

If these seem like startling images, we may remember that there are still folk hymns that describe faith in these erotic terms: "in the arms of my dear Savior, O there are ten thousand charms."[9] Mechthild thinks mercy and forgiveness are important but only as a way to remove obstacles to the joyous mutual love between the Soul and divine Love. By itself, forgiveness remains extrinsic to the deepest reality of the human soul. We are not created to be forgiven but to love and be loved. Desire expresses the purpose of our lives and the fundamental way God relates to us. Desire restores the fullness of loving connection. God's longing for humanity is not only the motivation for salvation, it is also the source of creation.

"Plucking the Holy Trinity:" Desire in the Celestial Court

The richness of Mechthild's theological imagination is displayed in the multiplicity of her images; each image refracts through a prism that together evoke the unquenchable love God has for humanity. In her hands, the metaphor of a celestial court governed by a divine king becomes a meditation on divine desire. Though it is the Father, Son, and Holy Spirit that conspire to create and redeem humanity, desire to do so comes from Lady Love who "struggled many a year before you compelled the high Trinity to pour itself into Mary's humble womb."[10]

Mechthild uses her poetic license to create a *mise-en-scéne* in which we are privy to the inner workings of the Trinity at home. The "perichoresis" of Father, Son, and Spirit is a divine dance in which each is perfected in relation to the others. The Father is seen in grand splendor, perfect in majesty and power. But without the interventions of the Spirit's kind heart and the loving wisdom of the Son, this majesty would remain sterile. Mechthild describes the Trinity adorned with different powers: Father with omnipotence, the Son with wisdom, and the Holy Spirit with compassion.[11] Flowing through all three is Lady Love, not a separate entity but the quality that perfects each power. When power or wisdom are not directed by love, they are not divine.

As Mechthild tells it, the story of creation begins when the Holy Spirit plucks the Trinity like a lyre. The Spirit sings to the Trinity like a court troubadour and offers generous advice. The Spirit no longer wants to continue on unfruitfully. The Son, too, wishes to bear fruit. By creating humanity in his own image he will "undertake wondrous things." The Son foresees tragedy but promises to love humanity forever. The Spirit and the Son stir up in the Father a desire that is rooted in the godhead but that the regal Father does not think of by himself.

The Father's omnipotence *by itself* is only barrenness or aridity that is alien to the deepest nature of the Trinity; pure power requires the prompting of tenderheartedness and wisdom in order to embrace the full potential of divine love. Awakened by the love of the Spirit and the Son, the Father recognizes a powerful desire stirring in his own breast, swelling from barren power into love. The Father promises that the Trinity will work together, becoming fruitful by making a bride "who shall greet me with her mouth and wound me with her [beautiful] appearance. Then does love first begin."[12]

Nothing comes forth from omnipotence alone. The Son and the Spirit play on the strings of love and awaken in the Father a desire for a beloved; breathing love into omnipotence awakens the Father to his deeper perfection. As love modifies sheer power, "wondrous things" emerge.

The Son foresees that he will die for this love, but creation begins joyously. Adam and Eve are formed with a share of the Son's heavenly wisdom and earthly power. The Father, in a divine version of marriage vows, bestows love upon the Soul and assures her that she will never be rejected.[13] The beloved queen, the spotless bride of the Holy Trinity, eats the apple and loses her angelic purity. The Father responds wrathfully, regretting his work, rejecting the "filthy" bride.

Here again the Son and Spirit prevail upon the Father, this time persuading him to renounce his angry justice. The Spirit and the Son conspire to unite divine perfection with fallen human nature by becoming incarnate in human form. The Son enters Mary's womb to be "sheltered for nine months." The Father again lovingly bows to their desire and joins the wonderful procession that rejoins divinity with humanity.[14]

In this beguiling of the Father, Lady Love is not a fourth member of the Trinity but the quality that divinizes the Father, Son, and Holy Spirit. It is Love that makes God, God. It is Love that calls God back to God's true self, to God's true motivations and desires, and to the most perfect execution of God's powers.

This story-scene shows God renouncing absolute power and wrathful justice. Without Love, power and justice are distorted, barren, and violent.[15] The self-emptying (*kenosis*) of Christ that Paul described in his famous hymn has its root in the Father's prior *kenosis* of omnipotence and strict justice.[16] There is here a subtle critique of human power and justice that are disconnected from love. The deeper truth of divine power is its boundless and self-giving yearning for humanity. For Mechthild, the drama of creation and redemption are bound up in divine desire. The Trinity creates out of longing for intimacy with the human soul. Incarnation and the passion are strategies to restore the bride to her original beauty.

The Flowing Light of Love

Like the troubadours who created beautiful poetry of love-haunted, tragically separated lovers, Mechthild evokes longing and surrender to depict the soul transformed by love, for love, into love. For her, love is not an extrinsic emotion of the soul but the site where the divine and human flow together. The godhead is a flowing light that transforms the soul into itself. Mechthild burned with a devotion to the Holy Trinity and her God-hungry heart was impatient with everything that separated her from her Lover. Flowing light, flowing love: God seeks the soul, hunting after her, his queen and beloved, "a desire of my Godhead."[17] The Trinity is a noble empress, beautiful, refined, rosy in the blossom of youth. She is the queen whose home is the human heart.[18] To an outcast beguine, Christ is her ready companion; because he has suffered, he is able to carry her sufferings.[19]

Through these images and reversals, Mechthild witnesses to the great beauty of divine love that flows unceasingly from the heights of heaven to the most humble soul. Where some church leaders envisioned divine power to be like their own, Mechthild's theology called the church and society to practices of redemptive love. She invites her readers to permit this love to flow through us toward all the world.

"The Ardor of the Spirit Has Such Healing Powers"[20]

We have allowed Mechthild to set the stage for us. Her theology of desire gives a sense of the vitality of devotion and the intensity of God's love for humanity. The God-hungry heart dedicates everything to the task of stripping off whatever stands between the Soul and Love. But it is also the soul-hungry heart of God that is beguiled by love for a "bride." For her sake, the Trinity takes up the work of creation and then redemption. Love does not permit divine omnipotence to be without issue. This emphasis on desire is present in Marguerite and Julian as well. Before turning to a fuller examination of Mechthild's thought, we will pause to listen to the echo of her words in these other two contemplative theologians.

Marguerite's use of desire is more complex because desire is both the pathway to God and also what expires when the soul is emptied into God. Desire is the last thing the Soul knows about herself before she is inebriated by self-forgetfulness. And yet "desire, will, and fear" defraud the Soul of the "highest light of the ardor of divine love."[21] The Soul "reduced to nothing" has overcome every will and desire so completely that they are no longer impediments between herself and divine Love. Love sings her praises: "such a soul can do as she pleases because her only pleasure is the divine will. She has crossed the Red Sea and her enemies [fear and desire] are drowned in it."[22] Egocentric desire is reduced to nothing, but as human desire is united with divine desire, it is ignited beyond all measure; it has entered into the infinite joyousness of the divine will.

The transformation of egocentric desire into divine desire takes enormous energy and courage. The soul approaching divinity is like a radiant star willingly disintegrating into a black hole. The energy for this is desire. Those who will make this passage will be enthusiastic and fiery, not lethargic, overly sensitive, or melancholy. It will be desire that enables contemplatives to envy and imitate the annihilated soul.[23]

Desire is also the last thing we know about God before theology disappears into "pondering nothing." The soul sings: "I say I will love him, but I lie for I am not. It is only he who loves me. He is and I am not . . . . This is the divine seed and devoted love."[24] But even this song of love is less than the love itself. The soul is perfect when it "remains in pure nothingness without thought, and not until then."[25] Because our desire is for something we cannot conceive of with our minds and which is less than our most ardent desires, Marguerite encourages us to employ the "intellect of love" and our "subtle understanding." As her evocation of this unity spirals to dizzying heights, she bids her hearers, the "ladies" that listen to her book, to "gloss these words," "attend to the core" and not the appearance. Even the most passionate words become a distraction from the reality of divinity. Relying on words *about* God is like trying to enclose the sea in an eye or carry the world at the end of a reed.[26] But until we fall into the silence of loving unity, it is desire that names the mutual yearning between God and humanity.

"Gladly and Merrily Because of His Love"

Julian, too, identifies desire as the heart-beat of faith that unites humanity to the Holy Trinity. This desire and yearning is itself so intense that it is a "lasting penance" whose pain will endure until the Trinity dwells in the soul. But desire is also a kind of connection. It is sweet; because of desire, we are able to bear our separation "gladly and merrily because of His Love."[27]

It is this divine love that precedes and inspires our own. Like Mechthild, Julian describes the efficacy of divine love by evoking the Trinity: the Father has the power, the Son has the efficacious wisdom, and the Spirit has the generous and good desire to create and redeem humanity. Love inspires the Trinity and inflames its desire to undertake any difficulty in order to draw humanity back to itself. But in all of this, the Trinity takes great "delight" in the soul "for He saw from the beginning what would please Him without end."[28]

At the beginning of her vision, Julian saw Jesus' thirst on the cross but she quickly understood that God's thirst was not for water but for humanity itself: "For the thirst of God is to have all humanity [drawn] into him, in which thirst he has drawn his holy souls that are now in bliss. And so gathering his living members, ever he draws and drinks and yet he continues to thirst and long."[29] This divine longing will endure as long as there is any member of the human body that remains estranged or cut off from the body of Christ.

Through desire, all of creation is united into a great and beautiful body. Its beauty has beguiled the Trinity and the Trinity will thirst for ever deeper intimacy with its betrothed beloved. Desire knits creation into a single fabric, the object of the divine devotion. Desire knits humanity back to its source, its love, and its fulfillment. Desire flows from one human being to another. Desire causes us to delight in one another's beauty and to feel compassion for each other's difficulties. We desire one another's good just as God desires ours. These desires—for God, for good, for joy, for union, for the beauty of creation created and restored—are all one desire. They are splinters of the divine desire, spinning off to dwell throughout creation. These desires are the threads that the Holy Trinity uses to bind creation back together and draw it into the divine heart.

6

"I Have Desired You since the World's Beginning"

Divine Power and Mystery

Mechthild is not a systematic theologian in the sense that Thomas Aquinas or Paul Tillich were. The genre of her writing is personal, visionary, and poetic. And yet, her focus on the priority of love provides a consistent interpretation of who God is. In exploring this theology, we will see how love and desire transform her understanding of who God is.

"I Have Desired You": Desire as Power

When Mechthild was old and dying she prayed for release from her bodily suffering and perhaps even more a release from her anguished longing for God. Her Beloved responds by acknowledging the divine longing for her is as eternal as the divine nature. "I have desired you since the beginning of the world. I desire you and you desire me. Where two desires come together, there is love perfect."[1] But for Mechthild this desire is not only a private love affair with her holy paramour. It is a clue to the divine nature.

Lurking in the background of our ideas about God are assumptions about power. If we think of God as a king, we are imagining what a human king is like and applying that picture to God. If we think of kings as arbiters of justice like King Arthur, we will imagine that even if the world appears unjust, the power of God will eventually restore justice in heaven and earth. "The arc of the moral universe is long but it bends toward justice," as Martin Luther King says.[2] If Nero is our model for kingship, we will imagine that God unpredictably metes out reward and violent punishment according to his whims. If we meditate on the scholastic attributes of simplicity, immutability, and eternity we may pass into imageless contemplation or drift toward a cold and distant metaphysical principle.

The church of Mechthild's time used monarchial images for God to justify a hierarchical ordering of human society: from God descended popes, bishops, clergy, lords, vassals, and fathers. Like medieval rulers, God demands obedience and loyalty. God's favor is to be desired and God's punishments feared.

Mechthild uses royal imagery for God (empress, queen, or lord). But because she conceives of power as a form of love, she understands monarchial metaphors in a distinctive way. God's majesty and omnipotence are qualities related to the divine desire for intimacy with humanity. For Mechthild, it is not sheer power that makes God divine. It is love. This play between love and power is evident in the preface of Mechthild's book, where God claims authorship of the book. "I made [*gemacht*] it in my powerlessness [*unmaht*], for I cannot contain my gift."[3] This is a paradoxical way of describing divine power. Even God is powerless to contain God, but the distinctive display of power is inspiration and a redemptive word. God is powerless to stop giving gifts to humanity. Because the divine nature is love, to do so would require the unmaking of divinity itself.

Theologians such as Augustine and Luther struggle to understand how to reconcile love and justice or divine omnipotence and human agency. This is in part because they think of power as coercive or univocal agency. But for Mechthild, God's desire for humanity is incompatible with sheer omnipotence, not because God has less power but because it is a different kind of power. God renounces power as "might," in favor of love. God is able to do precisely what God wants: create humanity for intimacy with the divine life and return it to that state when it falls. The ability to create intimacy is a different power than one that controls empires.

Surrendering to Desire

Like John of the Cross, Mechthild wraps her theology in love poems to God. She petitions God to love her passionately, often, and long. God answers: "That I love you passionately comes from my nature, for I am love itself. That I love you often comes from my desire, for I desire to be loved passionately. That I love you long comes from my being eternal, for I am without an end and without a beginning."[4] For anyone more familiar with hymns such as "Immortal, Invisible, God only Wise," Mechthild's holy pillow talk may feel disconcerting. But desire turns out to be a paradoxical evocation of divine omnipotence. Surrender to love and abdication of isolated omnipotence and enraged justice unleashes the divine power to create and to redeem. Mechthild uses the metaphor of surrender to make the theological point that humanity is created for intimacy with God and that when sin interferes with this intimacy, God has the power to override strict justice in order to restore it.

The soul in Mechthild's writings can be understood in light of her theology of creation and redemption. The soul's intimacy with God is not a private love affair but the destiny of humanity. Speaking to other contemplatives, she emphasizes that this intimacy is the point of all of their spiritual practice. In the end, it is not "works" that are important, but resting in this connection. In one image, the soul, like Martha in Luke's story, is distracted by many things, including good works and the discipline of prayer itself. But the Beloved has an eye on Mary, who chooses the better part.[5] Drawing the soul away from its spiritual toil, Holy Trinity "greets her in courtly language that one does not hear in the kitchen, clothes her in the garments that one fittingly wears in a palace, and surrenders himself into her powers."[6] Here the Trinity is like a great lord clothing a kitchen maid for a palace, drawing her away to be with him alone, without care or worry for her ordinary responsibilities. But in this image, the lord surrenders to the kitchen maid's power by relinquishing authority in favor of a loving relationship. The opposition between them melts away just as duality melts away between true lovers at the moment of their consuming desire.

Here, divine surrender is a way of evoking the non-dual quality of the soul in union with divine reality. Non-duality is not pantheistic sameness. It refers to an aspect of human awareness that is not structured by subject/object awareness. This awareness is not only a moment of ecstatic experience but also a way of disempowering egocentric desires and fears so one is more capable of love, compassion, and peaceful joy. Non-duality also refers to the aspect of divine reality that is not governed by words or being. God is not a being among beings, another entity in the world. This would make God more like a creature than the creator. The "surrender" of being is a way of saying that in unitive consciousness, the reduction of God to a being is dismantled. The various world religions have different ways of describing non-duality, but that this kind of awareness is appropriate to the nature of ultimate reality is found throughout all contemplative literatures.

God "surrenders" to unitive awareness. God also surrenders to the spirit of redemption. As all good Christians know, sin separates us from God and deserves to be punished. But in Mechthild's theology, God is like the priest at the beginning of *Les Misérables:* God surrenders the right to condemn and in this great mercy reconverts the soul back toward its divine origin.[7] Mechthild poeticizes this conversion as God's delight in surrendering to the mutual love between divinity and the soul. Mechthild sometimes describes this as God's surrender to her desire to free souls from purgatory. In response to her prayers, God promises to allow her desire for their redemption to win out over strict justice: "yes, when two wrestle with one another, the weaker will go under. I want to be weaker, though I am almighty."[8]

God seems to enjoy being cajoled into using God's power to free prisoners and absolve sin. In these images of divine surrender, Mechthild acknowledges that there is a kind of power that demands strict justice and leaves the guilty to languish in their prison. Those rulers, judges, and prison guards who have the power to torture or imprison exercise a particularly real and terrifying power on earth. But she withholds this kind of power from God. This is not because God has *less* power than these wielders of might but because that *kind* of power is a diseased and distorted power. Out of love, the Father abandons the power to perpetuate suffering because the deeper and more authentic power is what redeems, heals, and restores. Mercy is a different kind of almighty-ness which draws even those brutalized by sin back into loving communion. The kind of power that is revered and feared in human society is a fallen and distorted shadow of divine power. Mechthild uses the poetic image of surrender to make a theological point: divine power allows love to displace might.

Surrender is a way of saying that the divine impulse to redeem humanity is overwhelming and irresistible. Just as Romeo galloped across Italy to return to Juliet, the Trinity is overmastered by Love's compulsion to abandon majestic sterility. "When God could no longer contain himself, he created the soul and, in his immense love, gave himself to her as her own."[9] In this image, God is powerless to withhold God's power; God is enslaved by love for humanity. This metaphorical excess is familiar in love songs and poetry: the lover would walk five hundred miles or swim the deepest ocean or stand out in the rain. There are no mountains too high or rivers too wide to keep lovers apart. In these exuberant love songs, love is the extravagant delight of lovers willing to bleed out their whole being for the other.

From Mechthild's perspective, if our theology or spirituality is governed by terrifying images of a divine judge or jailer, we will not understand that this kind of power is rejected by God. The Trinity has surrendered to love and will stop at nothing to entice the beloved soul back. This divine alchemy resists direct description and can only be hinted at through a variety of metaphors. Surrender is a temporal metaphor for something that is always the case: the deepest truth of creation lies in the presence of God to the human soul, unimpeded by egocentrism, suffering, or sin. This eternal truth is damaged by the fall, but its fundamental reality is not destroyed.

The Coincidence of Opposites: Erotic Embrace and the Way of Negation

Mechthild's erotic images evoke a profound theology of creation and redemption. But these images are not literal descriptions. The Trinity is not a lyre to be plucked by the Spirit. God is not a king wandering into the kitchen to seduce a scullery maid or a wrestler throwing the game. In a paradoxical way, erotic images provide a pathway beyond images. Mechthild uses intense images to lead the mind beyond images. This can be unsettling and disorienting as one abandons the consolation of clear ideas about God for the nakedness of pure awareness. But however frightening it may seem, the soul seeking unity with God is only seeking its own nature: "A fish in water does not drown. A bird in the air does not sink."[10] Like a fish in the void of water, we fall into an abyss but discover who we are.

Theologians try to express the gap between human words and the mysterious transcendence of God as "Wholly Other" (Barth), the Good beyond Being (Pseudo-Dionysius), darkness and nothingness (John of the Cross). We cannot know what God is; we can only know what God is not (Thomas Aquinas). Mechthild's superabundance of intense imagery explodes the ability to cling to literal pictures. She insists that we "should love what is not, and we should flee what is."[11] That is, all of our images drawn from "what is" are less than the reality of God. If we attach to them, we are constrained by images drawn from creation that will always be inferior to the reality of the divine life.

Mechthild pursues this journey from image to imageless wonder in a series of dialogues near the beginning of her book. The Senses argue that what sense and reason teach are all that she needs. It is enough to practice virtue, learn the biblical teachings, and pray to the pictures of the divine we have in our head. But Mechthild rejects these as too limiting. They are the religion of children, while she longs for the religion of an adult.[12] The soul who seeks God abandons the senses, abandons the things of this world to go to the fairest one who dwells in the secret chamber of the invisible Trinity.[13]

These are wonderful, paradoxical images: what is most fair is invisible and dwells in perfect secrecy. Anyone who engages in practices of meditation will become aware of the limits of thought. Thoughts and emotions are like the visible part of an iceberg. They appear significant, but attention only to what is visible makes us believe that these mental images are all of who we are and believe that our thoughts are adequate to ultimate reality. Quieting the mind opens awareness to invisible and nonconceptual dimensions of mind.[14] In this interior silence, the soul dwells with the divine. As one contemporary author, Martin Laird, puts it, "communion with God in the silence of the heart is a God-given capacity, like the rhododendron's capacity to flower, the fledgling's for flight, and the child's for self-forgetful abandon and joy."[15] Mechthild evokes this silence and communion by describing a kind of divine bedchamber of the soul. With almost scathing intimacy, God bids her remove her clothing. The "clothing" that must be removed is not material but psychological: fear, shame, and external virtues. By abandoning sense, reason, image, and psychological obstacles the divine depth opens. "He gives himself to her, and she to him."[16]

For Mechthild, the human soul is a dwelling place for the divine. It is no small bedchamber but as infinite as the divine depths. Beyond the confines of the ego-mind, beyond the constraints of body and will, a mysterious luminosity opens in which same and other cease to make sense. Mechthild's ascetic practices carve away egocentrism so she can open to the divine center. Her fecund images carve away at the hold of reason so mind can dwell in divine silence.

Even in her day, literal minded clergy misunderstood her writings. Complaining of her critics' inability to understand what she is saying, she argued "one does not grasp divinely with human thoughts. Therefore they sin who have not opened their spirit to the invisible truth."[17] Restricting religious and theological language to its literal meaning—or imagining that language is adequate to the depths of divine reality—is as foolish as rejecting the light of the sun in favor of candlelight. And yet, the contemplative longs to remain in community with other theological writers. She must write and she must acknowledge the failure of writing. Writing is directed toward its own demise. "I have set down many a long description with few words. I say this to myself: 'How long do you poor puppies want to howl? You must be silent because I must conceal what is most beloved.'"[18]

Language deepens and communicates insight but also limits it. A deeper awareness of divinity requires an asceticism of language as well as an asceticism of the will. To know how to read theology or any spiritual writings, it is important to know how language works and to understand what it does. This is the basis of her frustration with one of her critics, her "Pharisee," as she calls him. The sin of her critic is to take language too literally. He attributes to language a straightforward quality that it does not have, especially in religious discourse. This misunderstanding about how religious language works is a failure to recognize its indirect, performative qualities. That is, language does not describe realities as much as evoke them. Vivid images drive the mind toward what is invisible and unspeakable. The work of language is to enable the mind to hold onto an image until it dissolves not only the image but the mental habit that accustoms us to rely on concepts.

Mechthild uses images, poetry, prose, visions, and dialogue to present a theology of divine love, power, and mystery. Hers is a direct challenge to theologies that deify might or terrify the mind with images of a divine executioner. Playfully and seriously, she argues that divine power is what restores the soul to intimacy with ultimate reality. Popes and kings are mere shadows of this. Too often their theologies project onto heaven their own fantasies of power rather than infusing human society with the lesson of divine love. For Mechthild and for all of us, theology is both inherently limited and indirect. But it is also important. How we envision divine power, love, mercy, or goodness will shape us and our societies.

7

"The Son of God Robbed Me of My Strictest Justice"

Christ and Salvation

Mechthild accepts the teachings of the church, but her emphasis on love reframes them. Like other beguines and women contemplatives, she is intoxicated by the brilliance of divine love and its relentless pursuit of sinful humanity. She believes that by participating in divine love, she becomes a vehicle of it. Through her, love flows from the godhead to humanity and back again. This free circulation of love is the purpose of creation and the result of redemption. In one sense, the pattern of her thinking would be familiar: creation, fall, incarnation, redemption.

The key to salvation is the incarnation. Christ's humanity provides a visible image of the invisible godhead. Through the incarnation, what is invisible and eternal condescends to the sensuality of human understanding. "The humanity of our lord is a conceptual image of the eternal godhead, so that that we can well grasp the godhead through the humanity, and like the holy trinity, hold and kiss God in an incomprehensible way."[1] Because what is in itself without form takes on form, we are able to understand something more concrete about divine Love. Also, by taking on a human form, Christ unites human nature to divine nature. This unity re-creates the intimacy between humanity and God, which was begun with creation. Because of Christ's double nature—both human and divine—the Trinity shines forth in all human souls; and though the soul is formed in a body, it has a divine light in it. What is sinful about human nature is purified by this reintegration with the divine nature. What was alienated is restored to intimacy.

Through his humanity, Christ loves and rejoices in his flesh, that is, not only the physicality of the human Jesus but more fundamentally, the "flesh" of humanity itself. Christ rejoices in humanity because it is his own body.

Because of her way of understanding the purpose of the incarnation, Mechthild does not interpret salvation as primarily forgiveness of sins. Salvation includes the healing of all of the ways human beings have become alienated from God. The incarnation therefore takes on multiple meanings for Mechthild: solidarity in suffering and persecution, mercy for sin, and restoration of the unity between divinity and humanity.

I Am Carrying Your Sufferings

Suffering is the most universal experience of human life, and it is a regular theme in Mechthild's writings. Although suffering can be a result of sin, she does not view suffering as deserved. Skillfully used, it can be a powerful instrument of transformation.

The disconnection between suffering and guilt is reflected in her choice of paradigmatic sufferers: Mary and Christ. Mary, "Lady, noble goddess above all pure humans," is sinless, but it is through suffering that her spirit becomes robust enough to bear the intensity of divine love.[2] She became human, gave birth to the Savior, and watched him die a heart-crushing death. Through her maternal anguish a fuller range of human suffering became woven into the life of the Trinity. Through her courage, the victory of love over suffering was given form. Mary's empathetic suffering and Christ's victimized suffering played complementary roles in the economy of salvation.

Because Mary and Christ share the suffering of humanity, they create a bridge of solidarity between God and humanity. Through Mary and Christ, divine power and wisdom are available in the midst of affliction. Because they suffered innocently, we can know that suffering is not reducible to guilt. Part of what makes suffering so unbearable is that it is, in addition to its essential painfulness, humiliating and alienating. It makes us lonely. Those who suffer much often feel guilty or ashamed or unable to believe in God. By disconnecting pain from feelings of guilt, Mechthild shows that suffering can be a passageway to deeper compassion and love.

As an old woman exiled to the land of pain, Mechthild describes precisely this rerouting of remorseless affliction to intimacy with the divine. She is restless and in pain, oppressed by darkness. "Then a revelation of divine love was given to me, in the appearance of an honorable empress. Her form was sweet, white and rosy in the bloom of youth."[3] The conversation between them alludes to the conversation between Lady Love and the Soul that opened Mechthild's book. Here again, divine Love encourages Mechthild and assures her that her pain will not diminish her but will be the road of heaven. Alone in the night, ill and in pain, Mechthild awoke to the presence of Love.

But even though she understands that suffering is not punishment, it still seems to her a difficult path: "God guides his chosen children along strange paths. This is a strange path and an honorable path and a holy path that God himself went on, that a person suffers pain without sin and without shame."[4] This "strange path" is granted to those beloved by the Father so they will resemble His beloved Son, who was also tormented in body and soul. When Mechthild complains that she is subject to scorn and persecution, as well as physical pain and poverty, Christ consoles her: "I am in you, and you are in me."[5] But, perhaps like most people, Mechthild does not find this entirely satisfying. She is a good guide because she is honest about her feelings of frustration. Christ gives her another teaching by using his own suffering as a model of endurance: in his vulnerability to raging enemies, shameful poverty, and violent death he trusted in the Father's goodness. He instructs Mechthild to do likewise.[6] This somewhat bracing encouragement disentangles suffering from shame and prods her to accept whatever comes to her with courage and confidence in the goodness of God.

Christ's suffering also provides a pattern for Mechthild to understand the church's persecution of the nuns of Helfta. During a period when church officials were harassing the nuns and depriving them of the consolation of the Eucharist, she likens their suffering to being imprisoned. She asks Christ, "'Lord, how do you like this prison?' And our Lord said: 'I am held captive in it.'"[7] Just as Christ was beaten in his innocence, the nuns should bear their persecution without sadness. Just as Christ entrusted himself to the Father, they can trust in divine Love. And as Jesus rose from the dead, they can be confident that they will follow him to heaven.[8]

In a mysterious way, God even brings redemption out of the atrocities of war. Contemplating the horrors of war, she is assured that God will win the blessed through this suffering.[9] It was not entirely clear to her how this works. But for Mechthild it was enough to know that what appears to be meaningless and hopelessly destructive remains in the hands of divine mercy, which can bring redemption even from horrible violence.

Mechthild may be best known for her religious ecstasies and erotic poetry, but her theology of suffering runs through her text from beginning to end. In some mysterious way God's love for humanity remains present even in mortal illness, persecution, the savagery of war, and spiritual anguish. But this solidarity was not the only function of the incarnation. Jesus brings to humanity the good news that our suffering can be transformed from meaningless and destructive affliction into a path to God. He also brings news to the Father of the fragility of humanity and renegotiates the respective roles of justice and mercy as tools for addressing the destructiveness of sin.

Justice and Mercy

Mechthild's thinking about the apparent conflict between divine justice and love is not theoretical but, characteristically, through personifications. She sees Justice as a man entrusted by the Father with judgment since the sin of Adam. But Justice complains that a woman has joined him, taking what rightfully belonged to him. Anyone who flees to Mercy finds a soft hand laid on them while Justice stands there like an "idiot." Mercy comes from the Son of God, who robs Justice of his rights. Where Justice would dispense appropriate punishment on sinners, Mercy consoles, heals, and brings joy to all who seek her.[10] The potential conflict between Justice and Mercy is resolved by the intervention of the Son, whose mercy both limits and reorients Justice. There is still judgment for unrepentant guilt, but Justice is able to focus on a gentler task. In the company of Mercy, his work is to inspire friends of God to live a holy life. Through this discipline, God's friends share in the purity of Christ's own life.[11] Justice is no longer limited to punishment but works to rebalance and harmonize the soul.

This tableau presents key elements of Mechthild's theology of sin. Justice has a role to play in the divine response to sin, but it is run through the sieve of Mercy and so serves her. Sin must be realistically addressed. Justice is the personification of this process. But punishment does not reflect the ultimate purpose of God. Mercy and Justice conspire to draw humanity into a holy life where they will be restored to intimacy with the Trinity.

In a forensic model of salvation, divine judgment is interpreted through the metaphor of the criminal justice system and its courts of law. God is like a judge who demands penalty for crime, though willing to accept payment from someone other than the criminal. On this model, God is able to forgive, that is, remit punishment, because Christ offered his own blood in exchange. This criminal court image is frequently used in many forms of Reformation theology (John Calvin was a lawyer, after all), but for Mechthild, it does not capture what is distinctive about divine mercy. For Mechthild, the deepest truth of our nature is that we are the beloved of God. Creation and redemption arise from the divine yearning for intimacy. But this noble calling is too difficult for us. We betray our true nature and consort with goods and gods less deserving of our affection.

The depth of divine love is revealed in the Trinity's response to this betrayal. Where many human lovers call down the worst condemnations on a faithless beloved, divine Love responds in an opposite way, by using the humanity of Christ to draw humanity back. Jesus explains to Mechthild that though he is part of the eternal Trinity, he also has a human soul. Through the incarnation he reunites human and divine nature, and through his passion he enters into solidarity with human sin. His innocent human body allows him to carry the burden of human sin.

Mechthild does not seem to think of the passion as required by the Father to atone for sin. But because of Christ's solidarity with humanity, he is able to remind the Father how weak humanity is and therefore how unfair it would be for a strong man (the Father) to fight against a weak and blind one (humanity). He reminds the Father of the special bond that exists between humanity and divinity and that it would be wrong to allow anyone to perish. In these ways the Son reminds "the Heavenly Father of his infinite love for the human soul." In response to these interventions, the Father awakens to his own love for humanity: "My soul cannot suffer to exile the sinner from me. And so I follow many of them a long time until I grasp and keep them."[12] Through the device of narrative and personification, Mechthild articulates a theology of salvation that emphasizes the unity of humanity as an object of divine love and mercy.

"I Shall Let No One Perish"

The work of salvation is a joy to the Trinity. Mercy is the chief attribute Mechthild associates with Christ and, though she mentions him less, with the Holy Spirit. Together they instigate the process of redemption: ransom frightens away demons, mercy transforms justice, solidarity alleviates the anguish of suffering. But the process of salvation is a complex one.

For Mechthild sin is not a violation of the law but a disease of the will. God can work on the will but cannot control it. Mercy and compassion enter into the breach; they are themselves a kind of power, drawing souls from the purgatory of their self-enclosure to the sweetness of the divine presence. Sinners are susceptible to the compassion of others: Mechthild's tears for them have their own efficacy. Compassion and mercy are infinitely available, but they must work on spiritual beings and not on inert objects. It is this, and not residual divine justice or anger, that creates the fundamental problem of salvation. It is the will of the Trinity that no one perish, but this desire must contend with the recalcitrance of human free will. This problem proves to be the crux of Mechthild's reflections on sin and salvation.

Humanity must accept the love and mercy offered to it. It must be transformed for love. Christ's mercy and solidarity, even his binding up of bloody humanity with his own blood, cannot suffice for salvation. The Father has been converted from the dawn of time back to his eternal love and mercy. The problem is that humanity is able to resist the ministrations of the Holy Trinity as it seeks the conversion of sinners.

Salvation as Sanctification

Mechthild does not live in a period when the Reformation language of grace versus works dominates religious thinking. It is obvious to her that the Trinity is ceaselessly and personally engaged in the mission of redemption. But it is also obvious to her that human beings have agency and are responsible for actions and their consequences. For Mechthild, the problem of sin is not that human beings are so depraved that they are "free" only to sin, like severe alcoholics who are "free" only to drink. Human beings have a path of salvation available to them. The Dominicans, beguines, and all holy Christians, show that it is possible to live a disciplined, charitable, and prayerful life. Teachings, practices, and communities are available that support the re-formation of desire. Human beings can become instruments of love and vehicles of mercy and compassion. They can become bearers of authentic and generous Christianity.

Wrongly directed desires for pleasure or for power entangle people in ways of life that alienate them from God. When they ally themselves with corrupt and sinful institutions and authorities, they share responsibility for the evil done. Because they are genuinely responsible for wrongdoing, sinners deserve their suffering. Mechthild's understanding of salvation has two primary prongs: the divinization that returns the soul to intimacy with God and the purgatorial process by which sin is removed from the soul.

Mechthild's understanding of salvation does not easily map onto the categories of justification and sanctification characteristic of the Reformation churches. In a certain sense, justification was accomplished when the Son, Spirit, and Lady Love converted the Father back to his love for humanity. But Mechthild frames this more as the tenderness and devotion of a lover seeking his beloved than a legal act by which a judge exonerates a prisoner. Her focus is on sanctification: the making holy of the human soul is the purpose of creation, which the Trinity will not abandon. The work of redemption requires interplay between divine love and the spiritual capacities of the human person—body, soul, will, and desire. In this sense there is "work" for human beings to do too. We can engage a way of life that contributes to the re-formation of our soul.

Mechthild understands the contemplative life to be active participation in the process of sanctification. By choosing salvation, she acts in ways that make her more available to the divine desire. The "flowing of the light of the God-head" draws her into the work of redemption. Mechthild's prayers are God's own love flowing from God, to the soul, and back to the Holy Trinity. To borrow Meister Eckhart's metaphor, through the love that the flowing godhead awakens in us, God is born in the world. Mechthild's prayers on behalf of sinners is God's own love carving another passageway for the work redemption. Love is what makes the Holy Trinity divine. It is the divine part of the human soul. Devotion to God allows humanity to be transformed into the likeness of God.

Self-Centered Awareness

For Mechthild, self-will must be completely overcome in order to become naked to the divine Beloved. This is why asceticism is so important. But it is easy to be put off by the idea of purgatorial renunciation of the will. It may be easier to understand her interpretation of salvation if we translate her language of self-will into more contemporary terms.

That humans—and all sentient beings—are preoccupied with the vividness of their own bodily and emotional experience is entirely natural. Contemporary Christians will recognize it as part of the evolutionary process. And yet this ordinary fact is understood by most of Christian theology, including Mechthild, as an obstacle to God-consciousness. The natural attachment we have to our experience makes us the center of our attention and even the center of reality. This is what Augustine or Luther mean when they talk about original sin in terms of pride or as a turning away from God toward ourselves.

Our own experience is so vivid that the significance of other people's joy or suffering can seem fairly marginal by comparison. Contemplative practice exposes ways in which we constantly privilege our own psychological and physical needs. From a theological perspective this egocentric focus disorders the entire soul. The loving soul "rests in God alone when they share one will and no creature is so precious that it can hinder them."[13] But mental or physical agitation makes this purity of love difficult to attain. If we remember that most people can be crankier, less patient, less reasonable when they are hungry or tired or afraid, we will realize that our bodies can bring out the worst in us. We do not typically think of this as sin, but it is the existential background of Mechthild's discussions of body and will.

Mechthild is acutely aware of ways body and emotion distract her, but she does not appear to be especially concerned with her own guilt. In this sense, she does not share the anxiety of someone like Martin Luther that somehow her practice, prayer, penance, and devotion are not enough. The frustrations of earthly life do not indicate that God is condemning her. The peace of mind that the Reformers sought in grace Mechthild seems to experience as confidence in the love of God. Nonetheless, her theology of the body and of self-will reflect both the intransigence of egocentrism and the possibilities for transformation.

The Body

Contemporary people may not think much about the particular ways in which the body itself serves or resists the spiritual journey. Medieval Christians in general and Mechthild in particular were keenly aware of the limitations imposed by bodily existence. They associated the tensions between a willing spirit and a weak body (Matt. 26:41) with sin and observed the ways in which preoccupations of the body could conflict with spiritual intensions. For them, the body was a demanding tyrant feeding an insatiable self-will. It is this rerouting of attention from the divine reality to self-centered experience that must be uprooted if the soul is to rejoice in its Savior and Beloved as fully as possible.

It is not that having a body is itself sinful: the body is created by God and is "good." It is further sanctified by the incarnation. But the body is the locus of intense experiences of carnal desire, fear, pain, anger, and hatred which drive people toward inappropriate actions. In addition to sins related to bodily compulsions, the body in its natural state imposes difficult emotions on consciousness. "Low spirits" and illness are natural to embodied existence, but they distract the "God-hungry heart" from its deepest desires and yoke attention to the body.[14] This is not sin, but it is a constant irritation to Mechthild and may account for her frequent references to her sickbed. If physical suffering could not be a spiritual practice, she would have had little time for prayer.

Even in meditation, the body limits the soaring of the spirit. In a somewhat paradoxical image, Mechthild describes the body folding its wings so the soul can ascend to its greatest heights. As long as the body is still "flapping its wings," the soul remains stuck. Perhaps we should imagine a murder of crows flapping around an elegant eagle and preventing it from soaring.[15]

Even at its best, the body imposes limits, forcing God to restrain God-self, condescending to the frailty of the human body: "Beloved Dove, listen to me! My divine wisdom is so completely over you that I therefore must order my gifts to you so that your poor body can bear them."[16] Our frame is too fragile to bear the fullness of the godhead flowing into us. For Mechthild, working with the body was part of the process of transformation. But when one abandons evil habits, the body receives her share of love. When love storms the soul, she also melts through the senses and even the body has its share, becoming "refined in all things."[17]

Contemporary readers may find a connection to Mechthild's reflections on the body by considering ways in which experiments with diet, exercise, or bodily practices can be used to enhance mental vigor and defuse the importunities of the body and its emotions. Certain kinds of diets can enhance mental clarity and concentration. Bodily practices such as yoga, hymn singing, or chanting can pacify distractions and invite the body to participate in the infusion of love Mechthild describes.[18]

Free Will

The paradox of redemption is that free will is required for love but it is also the primary obstacle to love. Mutual love requires a genuine capacity to shape our desires and our choices. But this freedom is also what becomes stunted and diseased through sin: we express our agency through an egocentrism that binds us to distorted desires. Free will, which makes relationship possible, also makes possible decisions that sabotage relationship. Notwithstanding the song made popular by the Temptations, even God cannot "make you love me." Human beings are not dolls or robots. Sanctification works on spirits capable of divinization but that are crushed and distorted by sin. From Mechthild's point of view, this problem is only made much worse by corrupt religious institutions.

God is faced with the paradox of creating beings with free will but then being restricted by the consequences of this freedom. Mechthild portrays the cohabitation of divine power and free will through a visual image in which sin is personified as a bloodied and wounded child. She pictures herself carrying sinful and suffering humanity to God to plead for mercy: "Alas I look at the child with a bloody heart and with weeping eyes and take it into the arms of my soul to carry it before the feet of its Father." God replies, "I will cure the sickness of this child. If it does not again choose to fall into death, it shall share the same nature as my beauty, honor, and riches, surrounded and permeated by the ecstasy of eternal eternity. Arise my dear child, you are cured! The free will that I have given you I shall never take away, for it shall be the measure of your dignity, just as it is of the saints, in the beautiful kingdom of heaven. Alas, this child still lies motionless upon its own selfish will."[19]

In this image, Mechthild is shown that God shares her desire that sinners enter into to the beauty and happiness of eternity but that as long as they are enthralled to self-will, it is as if they are dead to their own nature. This is not, for Mechthild, the end of the story. The Holy Trinity may be limited by humanity's free will but not by the thin sliver of time allotted us on this earth.

Purgatory and the Redemption of Sinners

Mechthild was a child of her age. That souls experience material consequences of the good and evil they did during their lives was as natural to Mechthild as our acceptance of a heliocentric solar system. Most souls are a mixture of good and evil, of pure and impure desires. These souls would be purged of their evil until they became capable of intimacy with divine goodness. She accepted the doctrine of hell, though God assures her it is sparsely inhabited.[20] Purgatory, by contrast, is a rich site for reflection on the dynamics of redemption. Her images of purgatory provided a method for what we might now call "compassion meditation:" visualizations that helped expand compassion ever more universally and non-judgmentally. In the next chapter, we will encounter purgatory again as a device for social criticism.

For Mechthild, purgatory allows God to acknowledge that freedom has real consequences without allowing those consequences to create a permanent barrier to love. Redemption makes every aspect of the human being—heart, mind, and soul—available to love. This may take seemingly endless time, but the Trinity remains relentless as it balances its desire that "no one perish" against the stubbornness of human freedom.

She does not seem to think God angrily tosses human beings into pits of fire. God seems to be unhappy about purgatory and glad to release sinners. But purgatory represents the fact that freedom, unskillfully used, results in suffering. Recognizing this is a painful awakening for a compassionate soul, God discourages Mechthild from meditating on this too deeply. But, being Mechthild, she ignores him. In one scene, "this person's spirit was so powerfully angry that she grasped the whole of purgatory in her arms. She . . . pleaded lovingly. Then God spoke from heaven: 'Leave that now! . . . It is too hard for you."[21] Nonetheless, a negotiation commences and in the end the Lord permits her to take one thousand souls. He bowed low to them, placing upon each head a crown of love, saying: "This crown you shall wear eternally so all in my kingdom will know that it was because of tears of love that you were saved nine years before the right time."[22] There is in this image a complex interplay between justice and mercy. In a mysterious way, fierce compassion has a redemptive power in itself, a power which God honors by advertising to all the redeemed that everyone in this group was saved by "tears of love."

In another tussle over purgatory, Mechthild starts out talking to God about her shortcomings, which do not particularly interest God. He dismisses her sense of inadequacy and assures her that it is her desire itself that allows her to participate in the divine nature. Thus filled with a kind of yogic confidence, she takes on a Christlike role to cajole God into releasing sinners: "You are truly mine . . . Now, Lord, you shall be today a ransom for those imprisoned."[23] Through the strength God gives her, she leads him to a filthy, horrifying realm, chiding him: "O Lord, how many are there of these poor beings? You are my real price of ransom. You simply must show mercy." God admits there are numberless souls here who had neglected spiritual life on earth. When Mechthild begs for them he concedes that "It was right for you to bring me here. I shall not let them go unremembered." Mechthild herself negotiates with the demons, asking if "this ransom" is not enough. The demons shudder and acknowledge her superiority. The Lord finally steps in and fills the sinners with joy and love, placing them on a flower-bedecked mountain where they find inexpressible happiness.[24]

Poetically speaking, Mechthild's compassion for others' suffering reminds God that he has forgotten some prisoners who are now languishing in purgatory. To transpose this into theological terms, we might say that it is through longing and desire that we participate in the divine nature. Desire unites the soul with the divine nature so that God's longing for humanity flows into the soul and ignites in it a fierce compassion for all who suffer. From Mechthild's point of view, this compassionate desire has its own efficacy.

Even as an old woman, Mechthild continued to mingle purgatorial and erotic images. Too ill to go to mass, she draws the Lord to her little bed, laying him down on her pillow of pain. She begs him to sooth her by giving her sinners in a state of mortal sin. "Leave me just this wish: that I might die of love in love."[25] Mechthild's own purgatory of illness becomes sweet as she refocuses her attention from her own pain to the anguish of hopeless sinners. In washing them with her compassion, her pillow of pain is transformed into intimacy with divine love. This is the point of salvation. It allows us to use free will to reorient suffering into compassion and makes it possible to participate in the redemptive and joyous flow of divine love.

8

"A Virile Vassal in Battle"

Mechthild's Guide to Ethical Practice

> "There is a threeness about you. You are well made in God's image: You are a virile person in strife. You are a well costumed maiden in the palace of your lord. You are a joyous bride in your bed of love with God."[1]

Our theology matters. Because of her theological emphasis on God's love and compassion, Mechthild thinks these should translate into our daily actions. The beguines were part of the reforming spirit of the Middle Ages that emphasized the importance of the "apostolic life." These movements emphasized the importance of imitating the way of life chosen by Christ and his female and male followers. Contemplative prayer, courage in difficulty, and compassion toward sufferers were ways of drawing the ideals of the first Christians into daily life. Aligning with Jesus' human life would be a pathway to his divinity. It is important for modern readers to recognize that this way of life was not a withdrawal from the world for private prayer.[2] It was a path toward spiritual transformation that was also an explicit renunciation and implied criticism of the "property regime" of the church hierarchy.[3]

There Is a Threeness about You

For Mechthild, imitation of Christ is ontological as well as ethical: Christian life attempts to reconnect lived experience to its created nature. Made in the image of God, humanity is a mirror of the divine. Mechthild describes Christ as the mediator, drawing human nature into the Trinity and the Trinity into the human soul. Christ's (human) soul dwells eternally in unsurpassed dignity in the Holy Trinity, uniting the invisible and timeless Trinity with humanity. Through the soul of Christ, the Trinity shines beautifully in all creatures. Mechthild uses the metaphor of a mirror to evoke the way in which humanity reflects divinity. She celebrates his marvelous works performed through the "eternal mirror" of his humanity, a mirror in which the divine sees itself in humanity and humanity recognizes itself in divinity.[4]

This mutual indwelling of humanity and divinity provides the pattern for human life. "Well made in God's image," humanity can be strong in conflict, beautiful in disposition, and joyous to the depth of our souls. Imitation of Christ aligns human desire with its true nature: powerful, beautiful, joyous. Mechthild believes that her voluntary poverty and contemplative way of life, her emphases on mercy and compassion, and her energetic social critique flow from the connection between humanity and divinity manifested in Christ.

"How Love and the Queen Spoke to One Another"

Mechthild's book opens with a dialogue between Lady Love and the Soul that appears to be a defense of radical renunciation of even the most ordinary and humane pleasures and relationships. In her narrative depiction of the losses she has accrued on the spiritual path, Mechthild echoes a theme that is commonplace in Christian theology and spirituality: it is only when "everything transitory [becomes] cold and tasteless"[5] that true love of God emerges. But it is also important to recognize in her litany of loss an insistence that the values that shape her social world are backward and upside-down. Voluntary simplicity proves to be a way to expose social injustice.

When the Soul protests against Love's robbery of her childhood, youth, possessions, friends and relatives, honor and riches, Lady Love cavalierly dismisses her complaints. In exchange for earthly pleasures the Soul is offered Love herself and may demand God and all his kingdom as well.[6] This is a familiar Christian theme. If we sacrifice pleasure now we will be rewarded later. But what is less familiar is the reversal of power and honor that is embedded in this exchange.

The dialogue begins reasonably enough with the Soul respectfully greeting divine Love personified as a noble queen. But it is startling to hear Lady Love greet the Soul as "Lady Queen." Love and the Soul exchange honorifics appropriate to nobility. But Divine Love addresses the Soul as her Queen, a dramatic reversal of the respect exchanged between humanity and divinity. Lady Love offers the queenly soul her whole self and an entire kingdom. divine Love is a vassal, offering her life and lands to her liege lord. She is Lancelot offering her sword to King Arthur.

By addressing the Soul as "Lady Queen," Love cedes her eminence. The price extracted from the Soul for this, however, is nothing short of everything in her life. Through renunciation the soul becomes empty of self-will so that the divine light flows into her. The poverty of her life disguises the enormous wealth of her spiritual life. The personified Soul in this scene is not only Mechthild, a humble, scorned, and impoverished woman living at the edges of Magdeburg's society. The Soul is the site of the eternal and invisible godhead. It is the longed for bride for whom the Father cries out at the dawn of creation who will "greet me with her mouth and with her appearance wound me."[7] In the polite salutations that open her text, Mechthild foreshadows the enormous nobility of the Soul in union with the divine.

Divine Love's desire for the Soul and the Soul's quest for its divine Beloved is the foundation of Mechthild's theology. In Mechthild's imagery, the Soul is both a knight-errant on a God-intoxicated quest and also a noble lady, wooed by Love. These reversals are key to Mechthild's theology and ethics. In this light, the kind of happiness promised by society is a pseudo-happiness. The prestige craved by kings and bishops is pseudo-honor.

The Kingdom that Lady Love offers the Soul is not a fiefdom over which bishops and kings might battle. It is not the Holy Land toward which mercenaries hope to slaughter their way to victory. Lady Love offers Mechthild, a person of almost complete worldly powerlessness, a kingdom that feuding popes and salacious priests do not even know how to desire. When feminine wisdom interrupts the logic of a masculine church, peasants are not dispensable nonentities but known and honored for their faithfulness.[8] Mechthild is not a vulnerable crank but Love's liege-lady and beloved. Her powerlessness opens a vast channel through which the "light of the God-head" flows. In this light, the Soul becomes radiant, like gold shining through crystal.[9]

These reversals of power and honor are not for Mechthild only the stuff of mystical fantasy. They are the foundation of compassionate action and of social critique.

"Each One . . . Should Compassionately Do Good To Those [S]he Knows to Be in Need"[10]

Mechthild's theology is driven by Lady Love, who plants a seed of compassionate action superior to the marvels of contemplation. Lofty words without compassion are useless; love of God that rages against human beings is without value.[11] We get some clues about how contemplation of Love translates into practical compassion in her advice to leaders of religious communities.

Mechthild begins with this somewhat formidable advice: compassionately and cheerfully "you should so transform your heart in God's holy love that you love each brother or sister individually according to their particular needs."[12] This care should be quite concrete. Community leaders should arrange for basic comforts of others. They should console the sick every day while being generous with material gifts. They should clean them, make them laugh, and carry away their waste. "Then God's sweetness shall flow wonderfully into you."[13] Notwithstanding her own asceticism, she insists that leaders should not deprive religious people of their food. Excessive fasting or stinginess with food makes it impossible to sing or study well so that true religious practice is undermined by ascetic stringency.[14]

The radical compassion she envisions as the heart of practical action cannot be generated out of a sense of obligation or duty. It is a heart-sense that makes it unbearable to be indifferent to another's need or to think of anyone as "below" oneself. In an echo of her trinitarian understanding of the soul, she suggests a threefold practice to support this radical compassion: detachment, which participates in the transcendent mystery of the godhead; compassion, which participates in the humanity of Christ; and desire to care for human need, which participates in the Holy Spirit.[15] In addition, she recommends that one dedicate an hour or so to undisturbed prayer. Though she is writing to people who live in religious community, the insistence that the wells of mercy and compassion are fed by prayer is pertinent to modern people as well. As many an overworked pastor or mother knows, this hour (or even twenty minutes!) is difficult to find. Yet without it, compassionate care can become exhausting rather than grace-filled and sweet. We are better able to convey love and compassion when we are grounded in the experience of being loved ourselves.

Her emphasis on compassion is not limited to behavior within religious communities. Even when little practical aid was possible, her prayers connected her to all of humanity. Prayer for those in purgatory, as we saw in the last chapter, was a frequent practice. She prayed, too, for those who persecuted her, hoping that her "Christian torturers" would yet learn to love in true holiness and that false-hearted rulers would learn to spare the innocent.[16] She prayed for the human flotsam and jetsam caught in the maw of war.[17] She recommended compassion for those nearest and prayer which stretched one's mind over all humanity.

Love of God and of humanity are not two separate things, as if one could love God but shun humanity. Compassionate action reflects and mirrors the divine image.[18] Love is not an emotion or obligation but is God present in the soul. When we love others with warmth, affection, and care for their needs, it is God loving them through us. Mechthild hears Christ himself insist that "those who know and love the preciousness of my freedom, cannot bear to love me alone but must love me in creatures; then I remain nearest in their soul."[19]

"Deceit Has a Most Fair Appearance":[20] Contemplation as Social Critique

In Mechthild's visionary writings, critique of the church is an aspect of her dedication to divine love. The state of Christianity was a source of enormous suffering to her. At one point, she places her critique in the mouth of a devil who notes that he is well served by those religious people—monks, friars, and clerics—who "look like angels" but actually carry out his work. The sensuality of clerics and their propensity for hatred and discord are useful to Satan.[21] But for Mechthild, these things were a sword of sorrow.[22]

As always, she takes her pain to God. She imagines taking up "depraved Christianity" and forcing Christ to look straight at the disaster the church had become. He bids her to give up; this problem is too heavy for her. Undissuaded, she lays the church at his feet. To redeem humanity from its fall, the Son became incarnate and accepted death on a cross. But now, twelve centuries later, the church requires a second redemption. Alluding to the creation scene in which Christ foresees humanity's fall, Christ recognizes the church as the eternal bride who he will take in his kingly arms. And yet now she is a bleary-eyed, hobbling, filthy, listless maiden.[23] Though Mechthild is heartbroken and discouraged, Christ promises to wash the church in his own blood, to protect the guiltless, and to continue to send messengers.

One of those messengers is Mechthild herself. Gazing at this crippled church, Christ declares that through Mechthild's book he "sends a message to all religious people, the evil and the good, for if the pillars fall, the building cannot stand. I say to you truly, said our lord, in this book is my heart's blood written."[24] Christ simultaneously recognizes in besmeared Christianity the bride betrothed to the Trinity at creation, the vulnerability of the church, and the significance of Mechthild's work. The Dominican editor who put together her writings for circulation quoted this passage as the book's frontispiece. There were those in the brotherhood who shared her concern over what was happening in the church and the importance of her outspoken criticism.

For all of the excess humility and self-abnegation with which she writes, Mechthild nonetheless accepts her role in calling the church back to its true mission as one conferred by Christ himself. She uses images that starkly portray corruption so severe that it has driven Christ himself out of the church. She pictured Christ as a vagabond, attacked by church leaders who should be dearest to him.[25] She overheard the pope rebuked for allowing the church to become a path to hell.[26] Her personification of God as Lady Love and her visions of the church's corruption challenged the core theology of the medieval church. But this was precisely her point: when pillars fall, the building they support also falls. Mechthild's theology is a message to church leaders that their exercise of power is putting the whole of Christianity at risk. Characteristically, she develops her ideas through visual images.

Purgatory and the Reversal of Fortune

Mechthild was tenderhearted toward sinners, but she was also provoked by the moral turmoil of her world. Official theology justified the divine right of kings and the authoritarianism of the Vatican by conflating the goals of human rulers with the will of God. But Mechthild did not imagine that what we see in history necessarily reflects the divine will. Purgatory makes visible the moral truth that the trappings of power can conceal. In this world, corrupt clergy and secular rulers persecute those who affront them, immerse themselves in carnal pleasure and yet continue to bask in the glory of their status. Purgatory takes this mask off and shows the corruption for what it is. At the furthest depth of purgatory, at the very mouth of hell, Mechthild sees "bishops, high officials, and great lords."[27] However mighty on earth, they will not escape the consequences of their violence.

Mechthild was enmeshed in a struggle for the identity of Christianity. Where we stand in this struggle has consequences. If we align ourselves with evil powers, however much they claim to be angels of light, we reveal the worm of self-deception and cowardice in ourselves.

Mechthild shows the high price of mistaken loyalty in a vision of a Dominican brother she had known some forty years before. In praying for him, she expected to find him ensconced in heavenly radiance, but he was not there. She finds him suffering in purgatory, where he attributes his difficulty to misleading church leaders: "Those who falsely appeared to be holy made accusations to me against innocent people. I judged them accordingly and had a sinful opinion of them. That is why I suffer these torments." As she prays for him, God agrees to accept his intent, if not his actions, noting that he had followed malicious people. "Then he ascended in radiance . . . . Had he not yielded to false liars, he would have entered eternal joy with no suffering. That he wanted to trust them was his shame."[28] She puts this in a way that emphasizes not only that he was misled but that he, in a sense, wanted to be misled. It was easier and more pleasant to believe accusations against people. Mechthild indicates that she herself was one of those he persecuted. Through this visualization, she indicates that one cannot excuse harassment of the innocent by appealing to misguided admiration and obedience. But she also avoids the temptation to demonize her opponents. The desire for the good, even if it is temporarily confused, protects the soul from utter ruin.

Truth, Deception, and the Complications of Faithful Action

The incarnation and passion of Christ converted the Father to the cause of redemption. But here in this world, Christ remains a pilgrim. Unbelieving Christians reject him, leaving him homeless. When Christianity itself abandons Christ, the situation becomes dire. The institution that should teach the path of holiness was itself in disarray.

In our own time, activist churches and political theologians "speak truth to power." Mechthild was not at liberty to be so direct. Constructing her political theology in a visionary idiom, she defended beguines who were condemned by the church. Her visions show that their mistreatment by the church does not reflect the divine will. If there is danger in resisting those in authority, there is even greater danger in being misled by trappings of power.

The church had lost its way, absorbing itself in sensuality and secular power struggles. It defended its spiraling violence with a theology of divine wrath. Those who offered a different interpretation of Christianity were condemned. Francis and Clare suffered the dubious honor of becoming saints even as their closest followers were silenced or charged with heresy. Increasingly harsh decrees circumscribed the lives of beguines and they were threatened with excommunication for preaching false doctrine. Contemplative women were forced to accept the guidance of parish priests who were authorized by politically motivated bishops. The desire for a life dedicated to prayer, compassionate work, and voluntary poverty looked like an implicit criticism of the church's opulence and so became increasingly suspect and dangerous. Though she was spared watching the triumph of inquisition, Mechthild saw enough to despair of a real resolution. In a sense, the pillars *had* fallen. And yet, for all of her dismay at the church's confusion, she remained devoted to the end. As she carried "depraved Christianity" to the feet of Christ, she was shown the importance of her voice. But she was also shown that Christ did not abandon the church and continued to love the bride of his youth.

Mechthild lived, as we all do, in a world where religious authorities "pervert everything that is good."[29] Trying to discern what is true from what is false when it is religion itself that is sometimes operating as a force of evil can make faithfulness difficult. Her visionary approach to social critique functioned theologically as a device for telling difficult and even dangerous truths.

Preoccupation with truth can be a pretext for persecuting heretics as well as calling out the deceptions of those in authority. Struggling to love and seek the truth is crucial to religious life, not least because we are surrounded by collective lies all the time. If we grow up in a racist community, we may casually accept the inferiority of another person and their thousand degradations will seem perfectly natural to us. We may have been brought up in churches that taught that despising immigrants, gays and lesbians, or people of other faiths was crucial for our own salvation. We must reject those whom God rejects. How do we find leverage critically to reflect on the church, its ministries, and Scriptures when these supposedly divine authorities are themselves implicated in evil actions?

If we apply Mechthild's logic, we would say that we are guilty when we accept lies and persecute those who bear the divine image. Truth is a spiritual matter. Even if our freedom is only partial, we remain responsible for the deceptions in which we participate. But this remains murky, and it is difficult to be sure what to believe. Mechthild seems to suggest that in the midst of these confusions we should remain dedicated to Lady Love, faithful to the mercy of Christ, and long for the goodness of the Holy Trinity. As she says, God will pay attention to our desires and motives, even if we remain confused about who is holy and who is not. This may not give us all of the correct answers, but it will keep us moving in the right direction.

My Bride in Your Waiting

Reading Mechthild of Magdeburg is a delightful encounter with a beautiful, passionate spirit. Her writings foreshadow the courageous journey into the divine darkness we see in Meister Eckhart or John of the Cross.[30] This darkness, beyond imagination and image, holds no terrors for her. As a fish does not drown in water or a bird fall from the air, the soul falling into the divine abyss is only returning to its own nature.[31] A naked soul, she is adorned with boundless desire which alone is capacious enough for her Beloved's limitless love. In this mutual surrender the mystery of union burns in secret darkness.[32] From the depths of this mystery, Mechthild returns to chide an erring church, comfort the sick and afflicted, and provide instruction in the interior and exterior practices of compassionate care. A virile knight and a beautiful bride, she tirelessly quests for the perfection of love.

9

"Love Overmastered Me"

Reading Marguerite's Book

> "When she was in the desert, Love overmastered her and brought her to nothing, and so Love then worked in her, for her, without her, and then she lived a divine life. . . . She found God within herself without seeking him . . . for Love overmastered her."[1]

Marguerite Porete is the most difficult of the three contemplatives we are exploring in this book. I considered whether it was wise to include her at all. But I felt that I could not be complicit in her silencing. Also, she is one of the theologians whose uncompromising courage, spiritual ardor, and theological brilliance conspire to disclose the full radiance of the Christian path. It is rare to encounter Christianity's distinctive emphasis on divine love and mystery articulated at full reach. However difficult it is to follow Marguerite, it is important to know that she exists.

Marguerite's dominant theme is the capacity human beings have for union with divine reality and the peacefulness that comes from this union. Like Mechthild, she will use erotic metaphors for union but her more characteristic terminology is non-dualist. This makes her difficult to read in part because it is extremely difficult to get one's head around non-duality. It is also difficult because Christianity's preferred metaphors are personal and hierarchical and there is some suspicion of non-dualistic imagery. About this suspicion I will here make only two comments. First, however potent and consoling they can be, to rely almost exclusively on metaphors drawn from hierarchical power relationships to describe divine being is socially disastrous and theologically idolatrous. The Bible itself warns against this idolatry in the second commandment and elsewhere while conveying the mystery of God through an almost endless array of imagery: not only kings and fathers but mothers, various birds, rocks, small voices, fire, smoke, wombs, wings, a bent reed, an old woman sweeping, a mutilated corpse, honey, hammers, love, untranslatable phrases, unpronounceable consonants, and countless more. A second reason her imagery may be controversial is that it seems to imply that human beings are "the same" as God. I am not aware of anyone who holds this view. Nondualistic imagery invites the mind to move beyond discursive reason and its reliance on images and concepts. Struggling with Marguerite's difficult language can be a bracing reminder that we should inhabit language about God with a non-grasping lightness.

These are difficult waters. Marguerite herself is under no illusions about the intellectual and existential demands she places on her readers. She gives a good deal of guidance to her readers about how they might try to read her book. Her book is itself an itinerary that takes the Soul on an ascent—or descent—into annihilating joy. We will approach her thinking by looking at different elements of her writing. This will only be a rough prolegomena to an analysis of her thinking, but I hope it will be one that invites further inquiry.

Faith and Love Rather than Science

Because talking about God is inherently misleading, contemplatives have a difficult time conveying their fierce longing and the wordless mystery they encounter. The transformations that occur on the contemplative path defy conceptual categories. This makes these writings easy to misunderstand. Marguerite uses metaphor, literary devices, poetry, and theological argument to convey what is beyond all words. She interprets theology as wisdom rather than scientific understanding.[2] Her writing not only describes something but also invites readers to participate in the journey. As one friend put it, to read a precious thing like this is already to begin entering into the reality it describes. By way of analogy, one might read Julia Cameron's *The Artist's Way: A Spiritual Path to Higher Creativity* not only out of idle curiosity but also with pencil in hand.

Marguerite gives two crucial clues for how to read her book: avoid merely intellectual understanding and train the heart for love. As Lady Love says: "I pray that you study with great effort and diligence of the subtle understanding inside you, because otherwise those who hear will badly understand it."[3] When Love is explaining nonconceptual awareness, she interrupts herself to speak directly to her readers, advising them how important it is to read carefully and avoid literalism: "grasp this in a divine manner," "grasp the gloss." The free soul should renounce the "poverty of [Reason's] council."[4] Though

Marguerite is a formidable theologian and reading her book makes enormous intellectual demands on readers, it is not through discursive reason alone that the book will be understood. Marguerite advises her readers to:

> Humble then your scientific thinking,
> Which is based on Reason,
> And put all of your faithfulness
> In things which are given
> By Love, illuminated by Faith.
> And thus you will understand this book
> Which makes the soul live by Love.[5]

This emphasis on the limitations of discursive reasoning leads to her second piece of advice, which is to practice love. One should not do away with reason altogether, accepting whatever muddle-headed nonsense one wishes. Love has its own wisdom. To be formed by love is to prepare oneself for a higher understanding than reason *alone* can provide. To learn with the "intellect of love," one must actually practice love.[6] The path of freedom begins with the twin love commandments. For those of us used to studying things academically, the idea that the *heart* must be perfected before we can truly *understand* may seem strange, but it is an idea found in early Christianity as well as in other religious traditions. In Tibetan Buddhism, before learning some of the more advanced meditation practices, one must take the bodhisattva vow. This vow expresses the wish that all suffering be alleviated and requires the contemplative to commit herself to the desire to relieve suffering as long as it exists. There are kinds of truth that we can only understand in proportion to our capacity for radical compassion.

Marguerite seems to have something similar in mind when she insists that the twin love commandments are an essential preparation before undertaking a study of Lady Love's teachings. Her readers must love God with their entire being and "neither do, nor think, nor speak toward our neighbors anything we would not wish they do toward us. These commandments are necessary for the salvation of everyone: a lesser life cannot have grace."[7] I admit, this seems a rather high bar, but for Marguerite, the transformation of understanding will require transformation of the heart. Access to the "subtle intellect" will call upon the full range of human capacities.

The Mirror: A Dialogue of the Soul

Marguerite's one work, *The Mirror of Simple Souls*, was written for fellow beguines and other contemplatives to present a path toward complete liberation from egocentric consciousness. The divine energy or persona of Love lays out a path that leads to the dissolution of the personal or egocentric will into the divine will. In this unity, a complete peace arises that the world can neither give nor take away. When the Soul becomes simple and free, it becomes a mirror of the divine goodness.

Marguerite lays out this itinerary through a lively debate between the Soul, Reason, and Lady Love, with various other characters occasionally popping in and out. The Soul is eager to advance and is irritated at Reason's plodding pace. But Love indicates at the very beginning that the book will be directed by Reason's questions.[8] Though the Soul can be impatient and even insulting, it is Reason's questions that prompt Love to clarify her path so that a religious practitioner can understand it. God may be beyond words but we are not. The Soul wants to bound ahead in seven-league boots, but, like most readers, Reason remains confused and needs more guidance.

By constructing her theology as a dialogue, Marguerite is able to give voice to different aspects of a person's mind. The contemplative wants to rush ahead and drink in the joy of union she so thirsts for. She requires instruction about how to accomplish this, but she is impatient and eager. She is able to jump beyond discursive reason, but she still requires words, language, theology, and practice to make progress. Love tries to convey the experience of the Soul in words, but these feel inadequate and confusing to Reason. Reason is frustrated when she tries to translate what she is hearing into church doctrine. Love assures her there is room within the Holy Church for contemplative wisdom, but Reason is not sure she can accept that. Marguerite captures some of this complexity by personifying different aspects of mind as different voices.

In our own time, it remains difficult for the different parts of ourselves to understand everything that happens throughout the life of faith. We can experience doubt or confusion that seem to destroy faith. Or we might have experiences of grace or love that are at odds with certain teachings of the church. We might experience suffering and abuse that are hard to translate into doctrines of sin and forgiveness. We might encounter theological ideas that unsettle what seemed like unquestionable beliefs. From Marguerite Porete's point of view, all of these struggles and confusions are lovingly held by divine Love. The struggles are real, but they do not mean that we are estranged from God or even from Holy Church.

Two Lovelorn-Maidens: The Opening Exemplum

Marguerite opens her text with an exemplum, that is, a little story that captures the central point in a concise story or parable. The story is like a scale model of her book. It describes two ways one might pursue a contemplative path. They are both noble, but only the second has the power to completely free the mind from the constraints of its imagination and attachments.

In the first version of the story, a noble and courageous princess hears of the great king Alexander. Inspired by stories of his courtesy and nobility, she becomes inconsolable because, even though she has never met him, no love but his will satisfy her. Alexander is far away in distance but is drawn so near by her longing that he seems to be within her. He is absent, known only by reputation, but the longing of her heart makes him the most pressingly real character in her world. She imagines what this lover, who had so wounded and saddened her heart, might look like. To console herself, she has a portrait painted to represent her image of him. Gazing at this painting, she dreams of her distant king.[9]

Marguerite admires the ardor of the princess but shows that the king is known to her only through hearsay and imagination. The princess is obsessed with longing and constructs an image to ease her frustration. But the king never appears to the princess; he is known only by rumor. She dreams of the king, but all she has is an image constructed by her desire.

Like the noble princess, the beguines draw near to God through their affective piety, that is, through images that represent not divinity itself but the semblance of divinity painted by their emotions. It allows them to dream of their beloved. They are in love with love; they dream of God created in the image of their desire. Marguerite recognizes these contemplative women as greathearted, noble, and courageous. But their dreams are not actually of God but of their own desire. To the extent that the church relies only on concepts that reason can think about, it, too, is in love with its own images more than the ultimate, imageless reality of God.

She then offers a counterexample. This one, too, begins with a princess in love with a far-off king of great power, gentle courtesy, and nobility. She, too, is troubled because he is so far from her. But in this case, *he gives her* a book that represents his love to her. Though she remains in a "strange land and far from the palace," she has received news directly from him.[10]

The exemplum concludes in the voice of the Author. God, though utterly transcendent, is constrained by Love to show us a path that is not just the imaginations of our heart. Like the king, God is impossibly distant from our ideas but, out of love, provides a path so divinity is present in some fashion.

In Marguerite's church Scripture, sacraments, and Christ himself were clutched tightly in the hands of the clerics. As Protestant reformers would later complain, Scripture was in Latin, and Christ's saving grace had been cut off from the laity. Like other contemplatives, Marguerite insisted that God is not restricted to this institutional mediation. Divine Love constrains God to continually offer gifts to bring the divine goodness near those who desire it.

The church serves this purpose but is not itself God: the church was made for humanity, not humanity for the church.

These two parables prefigure a central paradox that Marguerite struggles with throughout the book. God in God's own being is transcendent. We humans try to reach this mysterious goodness through the imaginations of our heart and mind and through the mediations of the church. The living truth of divinity cannot be captured by words, images, ecstatic experiences, or institutions. And yet, because it is the supreme nature of this transcendent mystery to be good, it is compelled to impart this goodness to all creation. Love is the name of this self-disclosing, self-communicating power of divinity.

This paradox, characteristic of all religious language, is represented by the contrast between a maiden infatuated by her own desire and a maiden who has received a message directly from the king. We do not have direct access to divine reality in images of God captured in words. A book, even one revealed by divine Love, is not itself God. But without this gift, the path to God would be obscured. We should use this book, and all of the gifts of divine Love, as pathways to God. But we should not confuse the path with the goal. Marguerite seems to believe that the problem with the church is not that it has doctrines, ethical teachings, sacraments, and clergy. The problem is that, contrary to its own theological wisdom, it acts as if these things and only these things were divine.[11]

Through her exemplum, Marguerite orients the reader to what follows. Reason, words, books are all we have, but they remain images rather than the thing itself. Life in this world is exile in a "strange land." But Marguerite's *Mirror* is a gift from God, given out of love, to describe a path to liberation. The book is a roadmap for the "princess" to move beyond the mediated, affective piety of dreams to the transformation of the soul by and into the Holy Trinity. The reality of God is not what is written down in words. It is the power of transformation.

The Lost, the Forlorn, and the Free

Marguerite's thumbnail sketch of two kinds of spiritual seekers is a mirror held up to her readers, inviting them to recognize themselves in the courageous and noble first maiden but also to recognize that there is another path available to them. Her distinction between the lost, the forlorn, and the unencumbered soul is a way of thinking about how all of these paths fit together in one Holy Church.

During the Middle Ages, Jesus' death came to be understood primarily as atonement for human sin that appeased God's anger or justice.[12] The church alone was able to parcel out the merit that was accumulated by Christ's sacrifice. From the church's perspective, salvation meant participation in the instruments of forgiveness the church made available: belief, sacrament, liturgy, penance, obedience, and so on. As we have seen, reform movements sprang up to expand the meaning of Christian life to include not only passive reception of forgiveness but a transformation of the heart. Most of these movements, including that of the beguines, did not reject the church but rather sought ways to live out their love for God and humanity more completely.

Marguerite believed that the goodness of God is pure and undivided; nothing can ultimately thwart God's desire for the salvation of souls. In that sense, no one is lost. She assumes that most Christians are satisfied observing standard forms of piety. When Reason asks the Soul what she thinks of these practices, she replies that they are sufficient and blessed. "And Jesus Christ, who would not ever want to lose them, has fixed them to Himself by His death, and by His Gospels, and by His Scriptures, there where laboring people are guided by the right way."[13] Those who repudiate the contemplative path are "lost" only in the sense that the fullness of freedom is not available to them.

Her book is directed toward those who want to but do not know how to move beyond the penitential practice and theology they have been taught. She feels compassion for those to whom "No one would tell . . . the truth about Him."[14] Marguerite calls these contemplatives forlorn (sometimes translated "sad") because they long for something that seems impossible.

Awareness of the difficulty faced by fellow contemplatives entangles her in another paradox. The soul reduced to nothing has no more desire. But one desire remains—to help those still struggling. In Buddhism, the enlightened one returns to the world to teach the path of liberation out of compassion. Her book describes a path that extinguishes egocentric desire and yet it is grounded in the desire to alleviate the suffering of others. "And so this mendicant creature wrote what you hear. And she desired that her neighbors might find God in her, through writings and words. That is to say and mean, that she wished that her neighbors become the perfect ones" described in her book.[15]

Marguerite alludes to the story of the rich young ruler to encourage her readers to undertake the journey to freedom (Mark 10:17–27; Luke 18:18–26). When the young man asks Jesus how to become perfect, Jesus first responds by listing the ordinary requirements of faithful life. This is all that is required. But when the young man says he already does this, Jesus looks at him in love and recommends that he renounce everything to follow him. Jesus is sad that the young man was not able to do this but remains confident he can enter the kingdom. The "lost," like the rich young man, are loved and saved but choose not to pursue perfect love.[16] Marguerite is encouraging the "forlorn" to accept Jesus' challenge.

We might understand these forlorn contemplatives by way of analogy. If you have not read *Little Women* you may know a film version. There is a scene in which the adult Jo is restless and almost beside herself. She is consumed with self-doubt. She does not fit anywhere. She is awkward and confused. She fails at the domestic virtues of a good nineteenth century New England woman. She feels like she is going crazy. Her wise mother points out that it is natural for her to be frustrated. She is stuck in a small town where her aspirations must dead-end against the assumption she will marry and have children. Her mother arranges for her to go to New York, where she becomes a writer. A world opens for her where her talent flourishes, she gives joy and inspiration to young women, and she finds her true lover. There is nothing wrong with being a wife and mother—or a content church member. But it is mutilating for ardent lovers to be told there is no other life for them, that their desires make them failures as women and sinners against God.

Two Laws: Holy Church the Little and Holy Church the Great

Marguerite's *Mirror* describes the freedom of the soul that is drawn into union with God. Love praises this soul "reduced to nothing:" "This soul, says Love, is free, and more free, and very free, and supremely free and in root, and stock and in all of her branches and in all of the fruit of her branches."[17] Though this seemed startling to her clerical readers, Marguerite insists that this freedom is the fulfillment of the Christian faith. She considers herself a Christian writing for other Christians of the truth that is available to them through their faith. She believes that the Holy Church is great enough for all kinds of worshipers. But Reason is not so sure. "O holy Trinity, says Faith, Hope and Love, where are these supreme souls who this book describes? . . . All of Holy Church would be dismayed by them." Lady Love replies, "Truthfully, [you mean] Holy Church the Little, says Love; that church is governed by Reason, not Holy Church the Great, says divine Love, which is ruled by us."[18] Christianity is a promise of the liberating power of love and truth. The church is "little" when it restricts itself to the rich young ruler, that is, when it limits religious life to obedience to the external rules of the church and to the kind of knowledge available to discursive reasoning, doctrines, and creeds. But the church is more capacious than this: it is a way of perfection in love. This more inclusive sense of religious faith is identified by Lady Love as "Holy Church the Great."

Reason tries to adjudicate the difference between what she is learning from Love and what she has learned from the church. "Ah, Lady Soul, you have two laws, namely, for yourself and for us: ours for belief, and yours for love."[19]

The Soul agrees. The sacraments make available the salvation Jesus desired for humanity. The law of belief is adequate for them. Anxiety about salvation need not torment them. But church the little not only requires belief and sacraments but say these are the only way to love God.

The Soul argues that to rely *only* on external mediations limits faith to worship of creation rather than the creator and is in fact a rejection of God. It is as if the first princess gazed only at the portrait she had drawn even when a love letter from the king himself had arrived. In true love, one does not demand proofs or external signs. The lover experiences the love from the beloved directly and trusts in it perfectly. But when one is in love with God, one realizes even more that words and doctrines can speak only of an image of God, not God's own reality. Through love, the contemplative is guided by the one who is "so strong He will never die and about whom doctrine is not written . . . for his gift cannot be given form. He knows, without beginning, that I would believe him without witnesses . . . Love is its own witness: it is enough; if I want more, I do not really believe him."[20]

People who seek God *only* in "words of men and scriptures" are subjecting God to their sacraments and works rather than using these things as a pathway to God.[21] Alluding to the story of Jesus and the woman at the well, she argues that this worship of God only in "monasteries and temples" is a rejection of the omnipresence of divinity. When the will is united with God, one worships in "spirit and truth" by recognizing God everywhere.[22] She explains to Reason: "I look for him everywhere and there he is. He is one God, a single God in three Persons, and this God is everywhere; there, I find him."[23] She is attempting to recall the church to its own wisdom, captured in the Second Commandment and familiar through church teachings that God cannot be reduced to anything in creation, including the church itself.[24]

This is a serious charge. She is saying that though divine goodness is sufficient for the salvation of all, the church has so conflated its own doctrines and practices with God that it has become a factory of idols, as Calvin would put it much later. It is worshiping itself rather than God. Her point is not that mediators of divine goodness are themselves idols: her book is one such mediator. But to believe and act as if things that can be touched and tasted and reduced to words *are* God, and so much God that we can find God nowhere else, is to practice idolatry rather than worship. She does not think that this idolatry has captured the entire church. Marguerite participated in a large community of fellow contemplatives for whom union with God was the goal and passion of Christian life.[25] Like Mechthild, she was part of a conversation about what the church could be.

For Marguerite, it is Love that provides an account of who God is. The Soul united to God is taught and ruled by Love. When Reason asks Love who she is, Love responds by quoting 1 John 4:16: God is love. "I am God, says Love, and God is love and this soul is God by condition of love and I am God by divine nature and this soul is it [God] by right of love."[26] Love is divine by nature, and the soul is divine by participation in that Love.

Has He Now Set End and Limit to the Gifts of His Goodness?[27]

Marguerite identified teachings of Love and the teachings of the institutional church as all part of one holy church. But she identified the kind of Christianity that is governed by a narrow, legalistic reasoning as "holy church the little." Marguerite recognized that this "little" church, like the young ruler, is held by divine Love. But it is a church that has exiled Love from itself.

This step in analyzing Marguerite's journey toward divine love differentiates different ways people can practice Christianity. It is a vigorous defense of the potential within Christianity to lead to freedom. One need not turn to heterodox movements (or, to speak anachronistically, to other religious traditions). But one must be willing to love and obey Love above all things, even the church if necessary. To obey anything less than Love is to prefer creature to creator. But when one does embrace this radical faith, one recognizes that there are no limits upon the graces and gifts that the Trinity make available to the Soul and to humanity.

10

"The Divine School Is Held with Mouth Closed"

Reason, Virtue, and Love

> Reason: Tell me, Soul, what gives you more joy?
>
> Love: It is this, that she has taken leave of you and of the works of the Virtues. . . . But now she has so entered divine instruction that she reads where you left off. But this lesson is not made in writing by a human hand but by the Holy Spirit who writes in a marvelous way and the Soul is the precious parchment; the divine school is held with mouth shut and human mind cannot put it in words.[1]

In the last chapter, we saw that Marguerite was opening a space where religion would serve Love rather than the other way around. The primacy of love ordered everything rightly. It made space for every kind and level of religious practice, and it held open the door to radical freedom. As Jesus taught the woman at the well, God is worshiped not on this mountain or that temple but everywhere, in spirit and truth. As he intimated to the rich young man, ordinary practice is sufficient, but there is a path to perfect love.

Nonetheless, Reason and her church feel more comfortable in a temple, engaging in familiar practices. As we continue our ascent with Marguerite, we will see how she understands both the usefulness and the limits of reason. Reason represents that part of our mind that uses concepts, words, images, doctrines, symbols, and language to further understanding. That is, it is the most familiar part of our thinking. It is also that part of the church that expresses religious truth in doctrines, creeds, and systematic theology. Lady Reason plays an essential role in the religious life, but there are types of awareness that cannot be reduced to language and concepts. When the church or the soul fail to acknowledge this, they become artificially constrained and cannot reach toward the fullest mystery of Love.

The other part of the human being that plays a crucial role in the religious life is will or desire—that part of us that chooses but also that part of us that is consciously and unconsciously drawn toward what we perceive to be good. Even plants seek out what nourishes them; human beings are perhaps unique in our ability to desire things that are not good for us. The Virtues are Marguerite's personification of that part of us that limits and disciplines our access to those things that are not genuinely good. But just as Reason can run amuck when it is disconnected from love or tied too closely to institutional agendas, virtues can become distorted and can actually block spiritual progress.

Love assures Reason that her law is not less than Reason's. God can do nothing other than good, and the person absorbed into God can do nothing contrary to that goodness. This is an arduous journey that traverses from the night terrors of works of fear through the release of its lingering egocentrism to the inebriation of a soul reduced to "nothing." Reason, who has been the Soul's loyal companion, must choose where its loyalty lies as the Soul begins to learn lessons not written in words.

The Soul Befriends and Departs from Reason and the Virtues

Reason, when taking the part of "church the little" in Marguerite's dialogue, believed that love was an attribute of God and a Christian virtue but that it was subservient to larger theological and ethical concerns. That church and state must run according to their own rules is obvious to Reason, who does not concern herself overmuch when these conflict with compassionate love.

For Reason, the more pressing issue is the strict oversight required by human sinfulness. Human beings are so eaten up by sin they must remain chattel to harsh mistresses. The Virtues goad unwilling flesh through disciplines that chastise body and mind into obedience. Reason does not believe that desire can be reformed and that these austerities are essential to "give the manner of living well to all good souls and without which Virtues no one can be saved or come to the perfection of life and those who have them cannot be deceived."[2]

Marguerite seems acutely aware of the negative impact of self-hating theology and harsh practice on contemplative life. Like John of the Cross and Teresa of Avila, she speaks to fellow contemplatives whose theological (and social) context is beset with violence. Like these later saints, she seems passionately dedicated in her effort to contribute to a more healing and healthy environment for contemplative practice. She puts her criticism of penitential theology and practice in the mouth of Lady Love.

Lady Love has a different perspective on asceticism from Reason. She acknowledges that the Virtues can train the Soul, but once Love dwells in the Soul, their work is accomplished. Egocentric pleasures and overmastering emotions dismember the Soul's capacity for love. Various forms of self-discipline, watching the mind, overcoming preoccupations with pleasure or pain can reform desire. When this is accomplished, the pedagogy of austerity is no longer helpful. To think of a kind of analogy, we might consider overcoming a bad habit or addiction. There is a period when this is very difficult and a terrible struggle. But ideally a time comes when we are not completely preoccupied with the destructive desire. We forget about cigarettes altogether. We no longer struggle to keep our temper or overcome our shyness. When this happens, there is an internalized self-control that creates a space of inner freedom from the thing that had tyrannized our mind.

Love believes that the Virtues become distorted when they insist that human beings are so diseased that reformation is impossible and that austerities must therefore be lifelong commitments. Virtues degenerate into masochistic practices that demand everything, heart and body and life. The Virtues withhold every physical or emotional comfort and view attention to bodily needs with deep suspicion. The Virtues never stop their demands, insisting that salvation can be obtained only through great pain and suffering. The mortified and exhausted Soul who still feels tied to this theology accepts all of this and even says that "she would be willing to be thrashed by fear and tormented in hell until the judgment day if she knew she would be saved."[3]

The Virtues torment the body through endless mortifications and terrify the mind with the ever-present threat of hell. Reason argues that it is evident in God's demand that the Son suffer so gruesomely, that only physical and emotional pain will release penitents from the endless suffering they deserve. Without penitential suffering, the Soul will not behave herself or receive the forgiveness the church makes available. The implication is that abandonment to Love is nothing more than wantonness, self-indulgence, heresy, and sexual impropriety.

Love argues that the Virtues have legitimate work, but they do not turn aside divine wrath. Like Julian of Norwich a few decades later, Love insists there is no such thing. Virtues can make us more susceptible to divine Love, but they do not earn us salvation or shield us from God's supposed rage. God is pure goodness. Salvation is nothing other than the knowledge of the goodness of God. This knowledge prepares the Soul to be the dwelling place of this goodness.[4]

The soul is made for love, not fear. The body was made to support the soul in its quest for God. The urgent desires and fears of the body may make it an unreliable ally, but this does not mean that the natural needs of the body are inherently evil. Love is a pragmatist. The virtues prepare the soul for love by unchaining it from anxiety and self-preoccupation. But when the virtues overstep their boundaries, they cease to do their good work. In fact, Love believes their harsh tactics compromise the progress toward love. She has little truck with strategies that maintain the soul in servile passivity. Terror and self-absorbing penance are not the instruments of Love; they do not lead to Love, and they conceal divine goodness in a cloak of anger. They do not empower the soul to love but distract her with duties, fears, and a sense of worthlessness.

Virtues: Love's Handmaidens

Marguerite seems to recognize that the harsh self-abnegation of penitential theology can be self-defeating. As we saw with Mechthild, ascetical theology views attachment to pleasure and self-satisfaction as a serious obstacle to contemplative prayer and the practice of love. Marguerite makes this point in a careful way. To transpose her point into a more contemporary idiom, we might say that it is true that natural egocentrism limits our capacity for love. But a crippling sense of worthlessness or paralyzing fear and anxiety may only be made worse by penitential practices. At the same time, religious experience can itself become a subtle retrenchment of egocentrism. Marguerite writes to people who have already renounced most of life's ordinary pleasures but who may be subtly attached to spiritual goods.[5] As we saw in the last chapter, the "princess" in Marguerite's opening parable was courageous and great-hearted but preoccupied with her own inner theater. But Marguerite wants to display the trace of egocentrism at work in this religious drama in a way that does not simply feed back into a theologically imposed sense of unworthiness. Holy longing and holy starvation are not the same as greedy selfishness, but they still focus on one's own experiences.[6]

When in the service of Love, the virtues can help tame self-preoccupation. Egocentrism here does not mean being particularly selfish or egotistical. It simply refers to the ordinary fact that we experience our own bodies and minds much more vividly than we experience anything else, even if we are religious people. This normal feature of experience is an obstacle to the radical love to which Marguerite witnesses. As long as we are more concerned about our own experiences, even our religious life will remain focused on the fears and desires of the ego. Ideally, ascetical disciplines reroute experience so it is less concerned with the ego and becomes more alert to the omnipresence of divine goodness.

Beguines needed models of what a healthy spiritual life looked like. We can think of motherhood as a way of imagining ways loving desire can veer into masochistic self-sacrifice or egocentric indulgence before it finds courageous balance and joy. A mother in love with her own mothering, whose children are fantasies of her own ambition and emotion, cannot be said to actually love her children. We would not think of a terrified, abused mother as free. A woman who raises her children with strict discipline but no affection is less than ideal. A mother who lacks self-confidence or self-respect cannot easily instill these virtues in her children. Like these different kinds of unsuccessful mothers, beguines struggled with religious fantasies of spiritual ecstasy. They might be coerced and bullied by clerics and bad theology. They might dedicate themselves to joyless penance or find themselves emptied of healthy self-respect.

By contrast a healthy, confident, and loving mother looks much more like a free person. When her child is threatened, she is courageous in her or his defense. When her child is happy, she is filled with joy. A healthy mother is sufficiently free from her own inner demons and the compulsions of fatigue or hunger that she can respond appropriately to whatever is happening. This ability to rise above the nagging complaints of body and mind is not mournful or self-hating self-sacrifice. Neither is it a principled renunciation of those things that are required for bodily, emotional, and spiritual nourishment. It is the joyous wisdom of self-transcending love. The virtues are doing their work well when they contribute to this kind of balanced freedom to love.

Marguerite does not use the example of motherhood. Ordinary motherhood can be pretty heroic, but it is not the annihilation of the will that Marguerite describes. For her, the soul that has really vanquished its egocentric will is afflicted neither by desire nor by fear. She does not need to indulge or torture her body. The tribulations of life hold no terror for her, and life's consolations, including religious ones, hold no charm. Such a soul "neither desires nor despises poverty or tribulation, neither mass nor sermon, neither fasting nor prayer and gives to nature all that is necessary without remorse of conscience, but such a soul is so well ordered by transformation in unity with Love to which the will of this Soul is conjoined, that nature demands nothing which would be forbidden."[7]

Her point, emphasized in the second part of this quotation, is not that love makes everything permissible. Love has so filled and ordered the soul so that it cannot desire anything other than the divine goodness. Nothing is forbidden to it because it does not desire anything that is forbidden. Reason thinks freedom is mere wantonness; but for Marguerite this hard-won freedom is effortlessly balanced, courageous, and peaceful. As Love tells Reason, such Souls are free when "Love dwells in them, and the Virtues serve them without contradiction and without labor of these Souls."[8]

Reason Asks and Is Answered by Love

When doing their proper work, the Virtues transform will and desire into Love. The contemplative who understands this will be pragmatic. She will not torture herself because she believes that pain is the only way to please God. She will experiment with practices to discern what contributes to loving freedom and what undermines it.

When ruled by Love, Reason, like the Virtues, has a role to play. Though the Soul is frustrated by Reason's slow-witted questions, Love accepts Reason as an aspect of the human being to be treated with respect and appreciation. In this mood, Reason perceives that Love is her highest calling; she wishes to be the handmaid to the Love-inspired Soul: "For I recognize that I cannot have greater joy, no greater honor, that to be a servant to such a lady.[9]

Reason is crucial to the entire enterprise of Marguerite's book: its teachings could not exist without its words, metaphors, and theological arguments. But as the Soul advances toward divinity's ineffability, she gradually realizes that all knowledge is merely created. God is greater than anything that could ever be said or written. Language is the creation of human minds and in this sense all speech about God is "more like lying than telling the truth."[10] And yet the Soul must acknowledge that her transformation was guided by the understanding she gained from Love's teachings. The very writing that the Soul so disdains is at the same time the vehicle by which the Soul is gradually "unencumbered" by desire.[11] The journey to freedom uses the ministrations of Reason to reach beyond what Reason can itself understand.

Reason herself acknowledged this paradox. She praises the Soul's fecund emptiness: "O sweet abyss, at the bottom without bottom."[12] But in the same breath Reason sarcastically calls her a "very noble [imposing] rock on the wide plain of truth." Reason tries to appreciate the Soul's journey but feels completely disoriented by her strange ideas. Unless one is also residing in this imageless abyss, the Soul's wild talk is nothing but a disorienting stumbling block.[13] Reason likes the clear, straightforward teaching she hears at church and is unsettled by news from the mystics.

The Soul is equally irritated with Reason and says that her constant interruptions have ruined the book. Even Love admits that Reason can do little more than speak to others equally limited in their understanding.[14] Through dialogue, they have sought détente; but as the Soul finds herself annihilated into Love, she and Reason find it difficult to communicate.

The Death of Reason

On the contemplative path, discursive faculties extinguish themselves in the realization of ultimate reality. Marguerite describes this in a tragic-comic scene played out as the Soul tries to relate the experience of annihilation to her annoying companion, Reason.

When Reason falls in love with Love, Reason wishes to be her servant, even though the flight of the Soul beyond her is troubling. She loyally tries to mediate between Love and those who define themselves and their faith in terms of ideas, beliefs, and obedience to the church. But when Love tries to describe what happens in the dissolution of the Soul into the nameless and imageless void of ultimate reality, Reason is so shocked she goes into a coma. In the narrative of Marguerite's book, this is the (temporary) death of one of its characters. Theologically, it describes the "annihilation of the intellect's habitual way of understanding," as John of the Cross puts it.[15]

As we saw, the Virtues are dedicated to overcoming the fear, attachments, and clinging that dominate human consciousness. Reason agrees that sinful thoughts and actions should be strictly disciplined by the Virtues. Both Reason and the Virtues conceive of the human person as constituted by this play of lust and fear. It *is* us, and we would not exist without them. Their job is to constrain will and belief so they remain in the service of God and the church.

Love thinks the Virtues and Reason have a worthy but insufficient understanding of how they are supposed to work. Any of us would be glad if we were able to consistently choose and desire genuine goods. This is what the Virtues help us do. But Love teaches that will and desire are also able to do something much more amazing. They not only can choose to serve God; they can choose to undergo their own extinction in order to be united with divine Goodness. Like water that dissolves into the sea, the Soul dissolves into Love. her Bridegroom not only loves her, he transforms her entirely into himself.[16] Love praises the annihilated Soul: just as fire draws matter entirely into itself so that matter becomes fire, Love draws the Soul entirely into herself so the Soul becomes love. They are now one thing.[17]

What Reason fears is, in a sense, true. In a Soul "reduced to nothing," egocentrism is no more. It has been reduced to nothingness, to ash; it has disappeared in an oceanic abyss. From the point of view of the Virtues and Reason, this nothingness is utterly terrifying. But the Soul does not cease to exist when her fear and her desire are pacified; only fear and desire cease to exist. The Soul is enthroned in peace in the land of freedom, which is ruled by Love.[18]

The consequence of this is spelled out by Love: when the Soul has lost and found herself in God, she no longer seeks God in penances, sacraments, creatures above or below, or in justice or mercy or understanding or anything else.[19] Religious people love God by loving the things that bring God near, as lovers cherish the letters that bring their distant beloved near to their memory. But when the lover is at hand, it would be foolish to read the letters and ignore the dear one. When Love is all in all, there are no special things that make divine goodness near. One sees with the eyes of love, understands with the intellect of love, desires only what love would desire.

This point is found in other religious traditions as well: the point of religious practice is not practice itself, but recognizing divine goodness everywhere. As the Indian philosopher Shankara puts it, "When a great soul has found perfect tranquility by freeing his mind from all distracting thoughts and completely realizing Brahman [i.e., union with the divine], then he no longer needs sacred places, moral disciplines, set hours, postures, directions, or objects for his meditation."[20] This point is echoed by a Jewish contemporary of Christ, the great philosopher Philo of Alexander, who perceived that to an awakened mind, God's goodness is recognized in everything: "When the righteous man searches for the nature of all things, he makes his own admirable discovery: that everything is God's grace. Every being in the world, and the world itself, manifests the blessings and generosity of God."[21]

But what makes sense from the perspective of the state of union does not make sense to Reason. Hearing Love's praise of this Soul, Reason is no longer confused or distressed but is shocked to death: "O God! O God! O God! says Reason. What is this creature saying? This is completely astounding! But what will those nourished by me say? I do not know what to say to them nor how to respond to excuse this."[22] Reason knows that there is nothing to say that will not sound outrageous and inexcusable to "holy church the little." The Soul and Love acknowledge that this is the case. "True, these are marvels, says Love, great marvels to them; because they are far from the country where they would practice in ways that would bring them to such heights. But those who are in the country where God dwells, they are no longer astonished by it."[23] Understanding is shaped by practice. If one practices in the way of Love, this will not seem so strange. But that is cold and bitter comfort to Reason. "Ah God! Says Reason. How does one dare to say this? I do not dare to listen. I am truly fainting, Lady Soul, listening to you: my heart is faltering. I no longer have life."[24]

The Soul, intoxicated by her new freedom, is not sorry to see Reason go. "Alas! Why did this death take so long! Because as long as I had you, Lady Reason, I could not freely grasp my heritage."[25] As the journey approaches the purity of annihilation, Reason is no longer a helpful guide; she has become a weight that holds the Soul back. In the final ascent and dissolution, the purity of divine Love enables the Soul to surpass Reason and enter into the fullness of her joy.

And yet, even as the Soul is happily dancing on Reason's grave, Love speaks to the Soul who has become "nothing other than Love," in the name of Reason. Since Reason is "dead," Love takes up Reason's task by asking questions that will help the Soul convey what is happening to her. Even in this state of union, an aspect of the mind remains to reflect on it. That reflecting and interpreting part, that part which continues to mediate between annihilating union and conscious awareness, remains alive and continues to speak and write.

Reason's Choices

Faith seeks understanding, as Anselm famously said. Marguerite has evidently spent a great deal of energy on her own theological education and is at pains to participate in the conversation going on in the broader community of "contemplatives and actives."

At the same time, reasoning cannot by itself unlock the secrets of divine Love. Restricting ourselves to what Reason can understand is "more like lying than telling the truth" about God.[26] Reason, or that part of ourselves represented by Reason, has a choice here. Reason can play her role and then let the Soul fly free into the region unconditioned by the subject/object dualism essential to reason and language but inadequate to the silence in which divinity dwells. She can accept the delicacy of her role as a guide and interpreter who must watch as her companion disappears around a bend. Reason can only dream about what wonders await her friend. On the other hand, Reason may insist that only a crevasse, a village of infidels, a thick fog bank is around the bend. She can trip the Soul, bind her feet, clip her wings, terrify her mind. She can say religion is no more or less than what the preacher says it is.

Reason is aware of its own limits; all of the world's religions acknowledge that ultimate reality transcends speech and thought. We intuitively recognize this when we recognize the gap between elevating experiences and scientific reasoning. We know that when we listen to a beautiful piece of music, or enter an amazing poem, or allow ourselves to be entranced by natural beauty, we are using some part of our self that is not controlled by analytical knowledge. We know that love for children, friends, lovers, or humanity is different from believing church doctrine. We can feel the trembling when we enter the unsettling world of Jesus' parables. Abandon ninety-nine good sheep to their fate to seek out one mischievous wanderer? Ignore the good, hard-working son to reward the irresponsible drinking, whoring, spend-thrift son? No. That would be crazy. Why does Jesus think these are good ideas?

We can choose to acknowledge this. We can appreciate what Reason can do and yet let our heart leap into an awareness that will always be beyond the grasp of discursive understanding. But since this is a choice, and in fact an ethical choice, we can choose otherwise. From Marguerite's point of view, it is a choice to obey Love—that is, God—or to renounce God in favor of human institutions and ideas.

It should be emphasized that the limits of Reason do not mean that everything descends into undecidable relativism. Within its realm, Reason has important work to do. The limit of Reason is on the far side of rationality where the mind touches divine Love. As we have seen, Love is not capable of anything less than divine goodness.

For Reason, this can feel like a frightening betrayal of the certainties and consolations that have nourished her so carefully and lovingly. But for Love, the choice Reason faces is no choice at all. She affectionately celebrates the different roles played by Reason, the Virtues, Will, Desire, and Soul in the journey back to the divine source. But Love, not Reason, is divine; they can do their work only if all these human faculties are ruled by Love.

11

"This Gift Slays My Thoughts"

Divine Love and Divine Emptiness

Marguerite's shooting star appeared with such brilliance, arched across a dark sky, and ended in ash. It is the ash of an inquisitor's fire, and it is the ash of her desire, burned to nothing by the intensity of her union with divine goodness. This chapter will try to discuss a little further the most difficult part of her work: the non-duality of a soul "reduced to nothing."

When I first read Marguerite I hardly knew what to make of her. I found that the only reason my mind could follow her even a little bit was because I had recently completed a twelve-week intensive study of the mahamudra practice in Tibetan Buddhism. This mind-bending metaphysics combined intensive philosophical study with very specific instructions for meditation practice. As I understood it, we were engaging discursive and nondiscursive modes of awareness to awaken to blissful non-dual awareness of the wisdom of emptiness. (I do not mean to imply I experienced this, only that I studied it). This disciplined integration of discursive and nondiscursive thinking and of philosophy and meditation provided good background for studying Marguerite's theological-contemplative evocation of divine non-duality.

And She Is So Dissolved into Him That She Sees Neither Herself Nor Him[1]

The rest of this chapter describes the Soul's ascent. Many readers may want to skip this section. But I feel it necessary to provide some orientation to her apophatic theology for those readers who might be interested. Apophatic means something like "other than speech." In the Christian theological tradition, it was assumed that there are elements of divine reality that we can say something about: God's goodness, love, redemptive power, and so on. But what we can say does not exhaust the reality of God. Those things that are beyond our understanding or thinking do not appear to our discursive ways of thinking. In addition to using names for God, it is also necessary to walk the *via negativa*, the "way of negation." Negative or apophatic theology reminds us of the importance of naming God and also unnaming or negating what we think we know so we can appreciate the glorious mystery and transcendent goodness of divine reality.

Marguerite is not the only theologian to combine theology and contemplative prayer. Most premodern theologians would have done so. Thomas Aquinas was in his practice a contemplative, though a scholastic in his writing style. Neither is Marguerite the only theologian to insist that God is beyond the categories of human thinking and beyond the structures of created being; virtually any theologian would insist on this. Everything in creation and the structure of creation itself is temporal, finite, changing, and made up of parts. God is none of these things; instead, God is said to be eternal, infinite, immutable, and simple. This does not mean that God is a something that is eternal and immutable. Eternity means that the category of time does not apply to God one way or another. Infinity means that the structures of finitude do not apply to God. Immutability and simplicity mean that the categories of change, whole, part, same, and other do not apply to God. Again, most theologians would acknowledge this.[2]

Nonetheless, my mind is structured by time and space, change and complexity, and so my thoughts about God are entangled in this same mental habit. It is harder to try to "think" a kind of reality that is not structured by time or change than to think of God as *something* that is eternal and unchanging. My mind is structured by the difference between me and the world around me, that is, by the difference between subjects and objects. When I think about God, I think of God as an object, a something different from me.

Marguerite does not allow her readers to do this. Like any good theologian, she insists that God is not a thing, an entity with certain features. That would make God something in creation and not the Creator. Marguerite uses language to force her reader to enter into this non-thing, beyond being, unknowing, learned ignorance.[3] Her readers should not only understand that God is not a thing; they should also come away with the structures of their minds rearranged so that some glimmering of awareness emerges; her readers should begin to taste a kind of reality that is not a being.

Discursive reason is structured by being. This is very useful for thinking and communicating. But it cannot think beyond-being. The dismantling of discursive reason is not necessarily pleasant. The will is structured by attraction and aversion. This is extremely useful for sentient beings, drawing them toward what is good for them and turning them away from what is harmful. The dismantling of this kind of will is also not very pleasant. But for Marguerite, it is when discursive reasoning and egocentric desire are undone that the reality of eternal, infinite, unchanging, beyond-being goodness can touch the human mind and restore the human heart to the peace and joy for which it was created. This undoing is the "Ames Adnienties"—the Soul brought to nothing or annihilated. It is "unencumbered" by desire, fear, and concepts.

These ideas are not unique to her. But the combination of her theological brilliance and her contemplative realizations make her able to describe it with an integrity and consistency that is unusual. I suspect that her exclusion from the educated brotherhood of monks and clergy also helped. She was not formed by the same institutional assumptions that shape their theology. Even the great theologians refuse to draw the logical conclusion that institutions cannot demand an allegiance that belongs only to God. Protestants do not resolve this; they only transfer primary loyalty from the Roman Catholic hierarchy to their own institutional authorities and written words. Their bitter feuds over doctrine show how little they accept the limitations imposed by original sin they themselves describe. Doctrines are of necessity the best human minds can conceive but still shaped not only by human intelligence but also by institutional power struggles. By virtue of her marginal status, Marguerite is not so deeply formed by scholasticism or institutional politics. Her thinking is not confined by an allegiance to institutions that might bring her into conflict with divine Love.

The very things that make her able to follow the theological consequences of the negative way make her unsettling in the history of the church and of theology. The language of non-duality can make some readers think that she is saying that God is the *same as* the soul. But "sameness" only applies to beings. A mode of reality that is not an object, not a creature or a being cannot be described in language shaped by the duality between subjects and objects.[4]

For many Christians it is crucial to maintain the rigid difference between God and creation. Non-duality sounds like a challenge to this difference. From the perspective of someone like Marguerite, an insistence on the complete otherness of God is tainted by what appears to be the reduction of divine reality to an entity: that is, it seems to imply God is some sort of *thing* that is *other from* creation. This risks making God something more like a creature, just a very different one. It seems to undermine the more complete sense in which divinity is other, that is, otherwise than being and beyond essence. In this "otherwise," the distinction between same and different does not make sense.

The insistence on the difference between God and humanity also implies that a human being is an entity: that is, in its deepest reality, it is a thing, a being. However, contemplative awareness suggests a different understanding of what a human being is: soul, on this view, is not a thing but rather the capacity to be aware of reality. It is that part of us made in the image of God, made for communion with God, made to delight and enjoy God forever. But since God is not a thing, this mode of awareness—made in the image of God—cannot be a thing. Neither God nor the soul are essences or entities.

"Now Hear and Envy the Great Perfection of These Souls Brought to Nothing"[5]

Marguerite's book is not for the faint of heart. But even for those of us who cannot follow her, watching the journey is intoxicating. She understands that only a few will be drawn to the path she describes; her primary audience is those ardent souls who recognize this path as news of their longed-for Beloved.[6] The *Mirror* tracks the Soul as it becomes gradually more naked to the annihilating intensity of divine goodness. She summarizes this process in seven stages by which the Soul becomes nothing.[7]

First Stage

The first stage is the practice of the twin love commandment.[8] Marguerite understands that to truly practice this commandment requires the grace to be freed from sin. Or put another way, sin is the inability to love. Until one's entire heart is taken up with genuine affection, devotion, and adoration of God, this commandment lies inert. Until the heart burns with such compassion for all of humanity that one can no longer conceive of a desire to harm anyone, one is not really ready to enter more deeply into the life of prayer. Marguerite places love at the beginning and at the end of the way of perfection. It is both path and goal that re-anchors the Soul in true religion.

Love of God and neighbor is so familiar that it might seem banal, but it is actually very difficult. We might see it in a new light if we compare it to the Buddhist "way of the bodhisattva."[9] The bodhisattva is one who is motivated to seek enlightenment because he or she wishes to help all beings become free from suffering. This is a modest and attainable beginning. It is possible to wish that others do not suffer, and in our better moments we can, theoretically, wish this for people we do not know. On the basis of this wish, our hearts begin to soften and change so that it gradually changes into an intention. As this wish becomes more stable, one realizes that it is necessary to extinguish egocentric patterns and deceptive conceptual habits. A simple compassionate wish becomes the basis of the path to complete awakening.

As three-year-olds in Sunday school we learn that Jesus loves the little children, and so should we. Someone at the first stage perceives that the depth and scope of this love would require a thousand years to perfect.[10] And yet love is only the precondition of all genuine spiritual practice.

Second Stage

Notwithstanding the seeming impossibility of perfecting even this simple commandment, Marguerite encourages readers of noble courage not to fear to climb higher. Noticing that the love commandment is thwarted by egocentric preoccupations, at the second stage the Soul undertakes a life of evangelical poverty. This life renounces ordinary pleasures, giving to the flesh nothing that it desires. The Soul learns to despise material wealth, honor, and all of the ego's delights. The Soul must overcome the fear of loss, danger, and bodily weakness. As long as the Soul remains preoccupied with fear and desire, she cannot focus on her divine lover.

Third Stage

When fear and pleasure are sufficiently pacified, the Soul is able to genuinely enjoy good works. But this very enjoyment is itself another attachment. In the spiritual life, one attempts to will what God wills. But Marguerite argues that willing something—anything at all—is still *our* will. Even if the Soul desires good things, *even if she is desiring God*, she is still absorbed in her own will. Because the desire for God is still not-God, the desire for God can itself prove to be an obstacle. The will must abolish not only desires for what is less than God or even desire for God. It must abolish desire itself. Having seemingly given everything to God, the Soul realizes that if she does not give to God her desire for good works she is still holding something of herself back. Marguerite describes this martyrdom and sacrifice as very painful: mortifying the body is nothing compared to mortifying the spirit. But she insists that this bruising and breaking of herself enlarges the Soul for Love.[11]

Marguerite is surfacing the way love of God is a subtle form of self-love. Our virtuous actions and sacrifices are activities of the inner theater of our mind. She is not mocking this. She admires the "forlorn" who are in love with Christ and devoted to good works. She sympathizes with the emotions and affections of the lovelorn beguines to whom she writes. But she bracingly points out that spiritual emotions are still fundamentally egocentric. "But understand it well, it is herself that she loves, without her knowing and without her perceiving it. And those deceive themselves who love by the tenderness of their affection which prevents them from coming to understanding."[12]

Fourth Stage

The fourth stage focuses on meditation and contemplation. Here, too, Marguerite exposes the subtle deceptions that occur as one continues to progress on the contemplative path. Even after relatively little practice, meditation can begin to produce wonderful effects. Scientists point out that it triggers a relaxation response; it makes bodies feel better and minds less anxious. Reading the literature of more serious contemplatives, it becomes clear that experiences of deep joy and profound insight are commonplace as one advances in these practices.

Marguerite describes bedazzlement by the divine light and love. The Soul is no longer practicing love as something external but beholding Love itself. This "seeing" is dazzling and overwhelming in its beauty and joy. Marguerite describes this as Fine Love carrying the Soul beyond and outside herself. A soul intoxicated by Love is powerless to resist: divine Love has overtaken her. And yet, while this is part of the transformation of the Soul into Love, the sweetness of Love can deceive those who do not recognize that there are yet further stages to be traversed.[13]

Marguerite's brief description is resonant with the distinction between meditation and contemplation. Meditation is a practice of concentration or focus on a word or a passage of Scripture, for example. Contemplation is the spontaneous opening of the mind to immediate and effortless experience of the divine presence. Many religious traditions note that contemplative practice naturally evokes blissful experiences.[14] Experiences like this can be genuinely helpful, empowering wisdom, understanding, or courage; they may be transformative or edifying. But they are still experiences. Marguerite is suspicious not of the experiences but of attachment to them as if they are ends in themselves.

Fifth Stage

After this inebriation by Love, the Soul is prepared for a deeper and more caustic self-knowledge. She has already traversed a great distance. Beginning with the ardor of love, she has become disenchanted with the world's pleasures and has pacified her fears. She endured scathing asceticism of the will and renounced pleasure in spiritual practices. She has been lifted up, seared, and dazzled by divine Love. She has displayed the lion-hearted fearlessness of a knight who has not been bowed down by hardship or distracted by meretricious beauty.

Stage Four united the Soul with Love. This is the unity that shocked Reason to death in an earlier chapter. Unity with divine Love surpasses what discursive awareness can understand. But it is only the manifest form of divinity. It is the last thing the Soul perceives before the way of unknowing begins to open.

Love is a name for God. It is the primary thing we now about God. But God cannot be grasped by reason or knowledge. That aspect of divine reality that is not structured by language might be said to be the un-manifest reality of God: divinity un-manifest to thinking, not-appearing in ideas or even "mystical" experience. For Marguerite, true and radical freedom is being grasped by the un-manifest power of divine reality. The previous stages prepared for this.

Marguerite describes the non-duality of union as the paradox of the annihilated will. Will and desire are both what makes union possible and what must be left behind in union. They are energies that make it possible for the soul to transform into divine Goodness, and they are the quality of soul that is susceptible to becoming good. This deeper penetration of the soul by God can only occur when will wills its own annihilation and desire desires its own nothingness. This is the purity of non-duality, where the "sweet abyssed one" falls into the divine emptiness. This paradoxical desire refines the Soul's subtlest impediments, so divine goodness becomes all in all. This is not the dazzling beauty of Love intoxicating the enraptured Soul but . . . but what? Language fails.

In the fifth stage God opens the mind of the Soul to the profound sense in which God is and the Soul is not. The Soul, as created and other than God, has no ultimate reality. In this sense it is by nature nothing.[15] But God has enclosed this nothingness, this not-God, with the gift of free will. The human being is a kind of existential nothingness into which the Trinity has inserted free will.

The nothingness that the Soul is shown in the fifth stage is the opposite of its ordinary experience. The Soul experiences itself as the center of the universe. This is what egocentrism means. It is the most natural part of human (or any being's) awareness. In Tolstoy's novella *The Death of Ivan Ilyich*, as he lies dying, Ivan Ilyich plaintively complains that surely someone would have told him if he was the sort of thing that would die. This is logically absurd but it is the existential centerpiece of human consciousness. Ivan cannot die because he *is* reality.[16]

Divine Goodness shows the Soul the truth that Ivan Ilyich so painfully learned on his deathbed: in itself, created being is nothing. But Goodness does not show the Soul her nothingness to bow her down with despair and futility. By seeing this nothingness, she recognizes the illusory nature of her ordinary consciousness. She sees that the fears and desires that have seemed so intransigently real are dust. They come into existence and pass away, leaving no more residue than the slightest dust mote. From an entirely different point of view, Carl Sagan also drew attention to this nothingness: "even these stars, which seem so numerous, are, as sand, as dust, or less than dust, in the enormity of the space in which there is nothing. Nothing!"[17]

The Soul is shown her nothingness and the illusory quality of all of her joys and sorrows that had seemed so real and oppressive. Desire and will are what attach the Soul to this illusion. But they are also the energy that will explode illusion. By recognizing this illusion, the Soul is able to desire to be free from it. Desire can thus desire its own termination. When the desire that holds this illusion in place is reduced to nothing, the Soul's infinite spaciousness opens and becomes available to the infinity of divine goodness.

The transmigration from illusory being to divine goodness can only be activated by desire. For Marguerite, free will is important because only desire has sufficient intensity and power to willingly renounce itself. "The Soul sees by the divine light that she must desire only the divine desire without any other desire and that is the reason desire was given."[18] Desire is the fuel that makes it possible for the Soul to undergo the alchemy that turns it to pure flame.[19] This is the sublime purpose for which God inserted desire and will into the soul.

Divinity is perfect goodness; this goodness carves out the resistance that the ego throws up against God so that the will not only aligns with the will of God but dissolves into it. Under the impact of grace, free will is able to will the way it is intended, that is, it relinquishes itself to God.

This death of egocentric preoccupations seems, to the ego, a terrible thing. Marguerite acknowledges it is a painful transition. But it is through this transformation of consciousness that the deepest desires of the Soul, freed from egocentrism, can be realized. Recognizing the nothingness of createdness and the sublimity of divine goodness "takes from her wishes, desires, and works of goodness. She takes possession of her freedom and rests in the excellent nobility of all things."[20] When created will and desire are reduced to nothing, a spaciousness emerges that is filled with divine goodness. Thought and action do not cease, but they are restructured by non-egocentric consciousness. This is true freedom.

Sixth Stage

The fifth stage opens the eye of the Soul to her true nature and enables her to desire the dissolution of her will. It is reflexive awareness of union, where the mind experiences union and also is aware of union. The sixth stage is a purity of awareness in which the reflexivity of consciousness pauses and "the Soul no longer sees herself . . . nor God . . . . But God sees himself in her."[21] Only God can see God. In this state of nonconceptual awareness, the "self" has been utterly pacified and all that is left is the divine aware of itself. Meister Eckhart, who had access to Marguerite's manuscript, uses similar language to capture the non-duality between Soul and God: "the eye with which I see God is the same with which God sees me. My eye and God's eye is one eye, and one sight, and one knowledge, and one love."[22] There is nothing to will and no "self" to desire anything. The Soul is in repose and freedom, completely at peace. In describing this purity of goodness, Love has paid her "debt" to the readers of Marguerite's book; that is, Love has fulfilled the promise stated at the beginning to tell how the "children of Holy Church" can attain to the perfection of life and of peace.[23]

Seventh Stage

The mind cannot stay in a state of non-duality. It vacillates in its ability to participate in each of these stages. As the mind becomes more familiar with the abyss-like goodness of God, the "throne of peace" becomes more stable. But however stable this awareness becomes, it remains structured by an embodied mode of consciousness. In the sixth stage the mind is "free and pure and clarified" but not "glorified." The seventh stage remains within Love, unavailable to understanding until the "soul has left our body."[24] Only upon death will the journey be completed.

On the Freedom of the Christian

Marguerite believed that love and nonconceptual goodness were ultimate truths about God. The deepest transformations of the Soul were not in the hands of clerics but of God. Beyond the mediations of reason, virtue, and the church, the Soul was abandoned to Love. She desired to teach this way of prayer and theology to those practitioners who felt stirrings the church would not feed and in fact actively repressed. She was compelled to share the sweetness of this freedom with others, regardless of the cost.

Marguerite emphasizes that her book was not for people who are satisfied with the teachings of the church. It was not for professional university theologians. Those who work with her book "with the Understanding of Love" may find guidance. "This book is not written for the others."[25] If someone finds her theology disturbing, she advises her reader to avoid it; it won't be fruitful. But the Holy Trinity assures her "Paradise will be given to them."[26]

The original ending of her book was a glorious song, a besotted incantation that passes back and forth between feminine and masculine imagery, between inebriated love and the emptiness of a soul brought to nothing. It is a song of freedom, celebrating her "freedom from captivity."

> Truth announces to my heart
> That I am loved by one alone . . .
> This gift slays my thoughts
> By the delight of his love . . .
> And divine Love says to me
> That she has entered me
> And can do as she wants . . .

I say that I will love him.
I lie, I am not.
It is he alone that loves me:
He is, and I am not:
And I no longer need
Anything but what he wishes.
He is complete,
And in this I am complete
This is divine seed
And faithful love.[27]

A Magistra for the Twenty-First Century

Marguerite remains a powerful *magistra* to those who find themselves marginalized by the church. For women who feel lost in the patriarchal imagery of the liturgy, her feminine imagery refreshes our own theological imaginations. For those outraged by the church's self-serving preoccupation with authority and prestige, she reminds us that "Church the Little," will never overcome "Holy Church the Great." For those who work themselves to weary exhaustion, she reminds us that the noblest work is to rest in the divine goodness. From this Sabbath, every good flows of its own accord. Those nourished by the church but who remain thirsty for more may find in Marguerite one of the greatest Christian yoginis and a reminder that the Christian path can be a path of perfect love and freedom.

Many find the church, its teachings and practices, its liturgy and promises satisfying and nourishing. It forms them for love and inspires their love of justice. Marguerite wishes them well. They have no need for her. But some have learned only a harmful theology from their church. Others believe that the contemplative path only exists in other religions. For these, she opens a door. Through this door, at an obscure corner of the church, hidden by untended ivy and weeds, a secret garden opens. Light streams in. We are welcome, beloved, cherished. Our wounds are bound up. Our worries and frustrations are soothed. A peace opens in the depth of our heart. Effortlessly and spontaneously, we radiate a brilliant light of love that caresses every being. We do nothing, and yet everything is accomplished.

12

"Who Shall Teach Me What I Need to Know?"

Fall and Redemption in Julian's Vision

> "I wept inwardly with all my might. . . . Ah, lord Jesus, King of bliss, how shall I be made easy? Who shall tell me and teach me what I need to know, if I may not at this time see it in you?"[1]

As we turn to Julian, we find another woman tormented by the irreconcilable difference between what she is taught by the church and what she experiences of divine love. For Julian, this tension is exacerbated by the predominance of suffering around her. She wrote during one of the most violent and unstable periods of Western history. Coming to terms with suffering and sin is the central concern that animates her writing.

The revelations ("showings") that give shape to her theology begin with the bleeding face of Jesus. The hideousness of human evil is beheld by her in the grotesque face of the crucified Christ. Jesus' beloved face is the "fairest of heaven." But she sees it hideously disfigured by blood and pain and by the "likeness of our foul, black dead covering."[2] This is the root of her insight. The beauty of the divine life has entered into humanity's disfiguring pain. The presence of this divine beauty in our midst foreshadows the transformation of hideous sin and suffering into divine light. Even in our brutal disfigurement, Christ and the whole Trinity adores us without the slightest hint of blame or condemnation. Love is the eternal truth of the Holy Trinity, and we will never be parted from it.

Julian's life's work was an attempt to reconcile the human anguish she witnessed, the church's teachings she honored, and the divine love that was revealed to her. However impossible this reconciliation appears, she remained stubbornly confident that they are held together in the unity of the Trinity's love. Scholars have different points of view. But it is my own view that this reconciliation ended by affirming the universality of salvation.

A Hazelnut

Julian's showings begin with intense scenes of Christ's death. But these are almost immediately interrupted by a "spiritual vision" of his love.[3] She sees that each human being is enwrapped in God's love like a warm cloak: "he is our clothing, that for love wraps us and winds about us and encloses us, hanging about us for tender love, that he many never leave us."[4]

A second image is opposite in scale. She is shown a tiny thing, about the size of a hazelnut, lying in the palm of her hand. She is told that "it is all that is made." She marvels that the whole of creation is no more than a tiny, insignificant trace, lingering on the edge of nothingness. But it will not fall into nothingness, because the Trinity made it, loves it, and keeps it. Divinity is without beginning or end, without time or change but is manifest as love. Because of love, a cosmos has been spun into existence and will be forever held in this love. This love does not come and go; it does not wax or wane. The creation, held together in undivided unity, is God's beloved.

"Knit and One-ed" with God

In Julian's theology of creation, all creation is held against the brink of nothingness by divine love. A second element of this theology is the creation of humanity as eternally united to the divine nature. Human nature is incarnate in the diversity of human bodies, but it is itself an ever-luminous, unstained goodness "knit and one-ed" with God. In this one-ing, we possess "a godly will that never assented to sin, nor never shall. This will is so good that it may never will evil but evermore continually wills good and works good in the sight of God."[5] Humanity is so joined to the Trinity that it cannot possibly do or be anything less than the divine image. "And I saw no difference between God and our substance, but as it were all God. And yet my understanding took that our substance is in God: that is to say, that God is God and our substance is a creature of God."[6]

Humanity in its essential nature is permanently welded to the divine, forming one substance: God as eternal, uncreated divinity; humanity as created being one-ed with God through God's love. All of creation is held in existence by the eternal act of divine love, and human nature is held in unity with God by that same eternal divine love. There is one substance that unites divine and human nature. In God, this substance is uncreated; in humanity, it is created. But for Julian, uncreated and created substance are one-ed in God. True self-knowledge is grounded in knowledge of God: "For our soul is so deeply grounded in God and so endlessly treasured, that we may not come to the knowing of it until we first know God, which is the maker to whom it is one-ed."[7]

But this eternal "one-ing" becomes individuated in the unique person of each human being: "diversities flowing out of him, to work his will."[8] There is no differentiation in the human nature united with the Trinity, but it is through the diversity and complexity of embodiment that humanity's full beauty will be displayed. Like Christ, though in created form, one part of human nature is eternally united with the Trinity, and another part is embodied on earth in individual persons.

The plurality and diversity of human beings is the necessary manifestation of human nature in time and space. In loving its creation, the Trinity loves not only our perfect substance but also our sensual selves. A purely spiritual and undifferentiated being lacks the capacity for self-conscious awareness or love. It is purely absorbed into unity. Humanity needs to be embodied in flesh, bone, emotion, and reason in order to know itself and to consciously return God's love. The supreme accomplishment of the Trinity is human being: individual, embodied persons that are so united to the godhead that we can never be separated. This is the great delight of the Trinity who has created this sensual-luminous humanity to be God's dwelling place; it is the most pleasing of all of God's works.[9]

However ugly human suffering and sin, God "does not despise what he has made and does not disdain to serve us even in the simplest need that is proper to our body in nature, because of the love of our soul which he has made in his own likeness."[10] Her theology of creation emphasizes the full scope of providential goodness: it expands across all creation, and it does not forget to care for the body's intimate needs.

I Saw No Wrath

Jesus has shown Julian that creation itself and all of humanity are eternally held in the divine love. The "great divorce" between good and evil is nowhere on display. Creation is eternally held by the Trinity's making, loving, and keeping.

But this is completely at odds with everything she knows and has been taught: it is obvious to common sense that history is overtaken by evil so intense that it is impossible to imagine its redemption, a truth graphically represented by the damnation of sinners. Julian desperately wants to know the meaning of this, but what Jesus shows her is completely bewildering. There is no angry father demanding bloody recompense: in fact, there is no anger, no sin, and no punishment. We look on some things as evil, but this is not what God sees. "Notwithstanding all this, I saw truly that our lord was never angry nor never shall be. For he is God, he is good, he is truth, he is love, he is peace. And his might, his wisdom, his charity, and his unity suffer him not to be angry."[11] Instead of abhorrent sins, the Trinity perceives only painful wounds. "For he beholds sin as sorrow and pain to his lovers, in whom he assigns no blame because of his love."[12]

Further, she is shown that God does not think of sin as shameful. As we will see, sin is a tragic inevitability through which humanity will become the dwelling place for the Trinity. The substance of humanity remains one-ed with God; the sensuality through which human beings become individually capable of returning God's love makes sin inevitable. Sin is accepted by God as an element of creation because God includes in the economy of creation a plan for transforming sin into a deeper capacity for love. Just as every sin brings pain, so all of this pain will bring a blessing. God has remedies to heal every wound and to transform them into honors.[13] The Trinity assigns no blame to sin, seeing only pain that requires healing. Just as God created everything, so whatever is done is part of God's own doing: "For there is no doer but he [and] he never changes his purpose in anything . . . [and] is always completely pleased with all his works . . . How would anything be amiss?"[14] Instead of wrath and blame, she is shown only pain that will be transformed into joy and honor.

A Great Deed

Julian does not see how she can hold together what she is seeing with what the church teaches. As the shattering implications of Jesus' teachings become more apparent, her inner turmoil intensifies. Jesus attempts to comfort her with the promise that all will be made well. He recognizes that we witness things that are so destructive we cannot imagine how they will be remedied, but what seems impossible to us is not impossible to God. Julian does not accept this vague assurance and persists with her questions.[15]

The church's "solution" that will make all things well is to restore the justice of creation by prolonging suffering into the eternity of hell. From Julian's point of view, if this is the case then "all things" are *not* well. Jesus assures her that God's desire will not be thwarted but will be accomplished through a "great deed" known only to the Trinity. "For this is the great deed that our lord God shall do, in which deed he shall save his word in all things and he shall make well all that is not well. But what the deed shall be and how it shall be done, there is not creature beneath Christ that knows it."[16]

This assurance should let her off the hook. She can remain committed to the teachings of the church but have faith that God has a secret way of reconciling these things that no one, not even the church, knows about. Jesus is confident that when she experiences this at the end of time, she will be satisfied that "all is well."

But for Julian this is not good enough! She perceives that *how* sin is reconciled with divine love is not a minor point. It is not a catechism question that she can casually repeat. It is the *very heart* of spiritual practice.

Who is she to worship? What kind of power is ultimately real? Who are the representatives of Christ on earth? The fundamental meaning of Christianity is shaped by the answer to these questions. In a mirror of the eternal divide between heaven and hell, popes of her time are engaged in a bare-knuckled conflict for power and wealth—a Great Schism that split Christendom in two. If the church's teachings were reliable, Henry le Despenser, Bishop of Norwich, crusader and "fighting bishop," is an excellent example of how God will make "all things well": brutally crushing peasant's protests, burning religious dissenters, and crusading against foes.

If we train ourselves to stomach the eternal torment of our fellow human beings, then we are also training ourselves to worship hatred, violence, cruelty, domination, and torture. Who, then, is the real object of our worship? Julian cannot practice her faith until this is resolved. Her reason is unbearably afflicted by this conflict because she genuinely loves the church and is devoted to it as the way God is present on earth. "I wept inwardly with all my might . . . Ah, lord Jesus, King of bliss, how shall I be made easy? Who shall tell me and teach me what I need to know, if I may not at this time see it in you?"[17]

The urgency of her request has been mounting for several chapters. She states her desire "that I could see in God in what way the judgment of Holy Church is true in his sight and how it is proper for me to understand it. In this way, both judgments [of the church and of what she is being shown] would be saved . . . to the extent that would be honorable to God and right for me."[18] She portrays the higher judgment as coming from her revelation and the lower judgment as coming from the church, the former being of blameless love, the lower of blame and judgment. But she would like God to reconcile these for her.

In response to her anguish, Jesus stops trying to pawn her off with vague assurances but shows her an exemplum—a tableau of a lord and his servant—that will satisfy her understanding and console her heart. "But notwithstanding, the wonder of the exemplum never went from me; for it seemed it was given to me as an answer to my desire and yet I could not fully perceive in it an interpretation for my consolation."[19] It is the longed-for solution, but it is so puzzling that she does not even mention it in the Short Text.

As she meditates on her visions over the years she receives two more inner teachings. After some fifteen years, Jesus recognizes that she still cannot grasp the meaning of what she had been shown: "Would you know your lord's meaning? Be aware: love was his meaning. Who showed it to you? Love. What did he show you? Love. Why did he show it to you? For love. Keep yourself in this love and you shall know and see more of the same but you will never see or know any other thing forever."[20] This is a big clue. But what she saw is so shattering, so impossible, so unbelievable, she still does not know what to make of it.

Some five years after this, she receives a third inner teaching. She is instructed to reexamine the exemplum from the original vision in every detail. It is an allegory of the fall and of redemption. Her exegesis of this parable is the key to what Jesus has been trying to reveal to her.

The Parable of the Lord and the Servant[21]

Julian is shown a scene in which a lord sits in repose while a servant stands reverently by, ready to do the lord's will. The lord looks upon the servant lovingly and sweetly, then sends him on an errand to recover a treasure hidden in the earth. The servant gladly leaps up and runs to do the lord's bidding, but he immediately falls into a ditch and is badly hurt. He groans and writhes but cannot help himself in any way. The servant is so consumed with his pain that he forgets his beloved lord and cannot see that he is right there with him, full of love. His inability to see or remember this love is his worst suffering.

Julian looks carefully to see if the servant's fall had been his own fault, but it was not. Already we see why she would be confused. Traditional theology clearly diagnoses the fall as a consequence of pride, disobedience, and wanton sinfulness. But here, it is the servant's desire to please God that exposed him to danger. As he dashes off, full of joy to serve the lord, he tumbles into a ditch.

This falling and failure meets no disapproval; the lord continues to look on the servant with tender love. And though the lord has compassion for what the servant suffers, he already knows that not only will he be restored but his suffering and hard labor will be turned into greater joy. The lord considers it only fair that he reward his "dear-worthy" servant for his sufferings far better than if he had never fallen.

This is Jesus' explanation for evil, and it completely befuddles her. But when she returns to the parable under the renewed guidance of Jesus' inner teachings she begins to unravel its complex and multilayered symbolism. She sees that the servant has a twofold meaning as both Adam and Christ. The servant is Adam and thus all humanity: "For in the sight of God all humanity is one person and one person is all humanity."[22] She understands that Adam/humanity is eternally "knit and one-ed" with God. There is a part of human nature that does not fall and is never alienated from God. But there is a part that falls into a body and history. This is the "ditch" that the servant falls into. Though human beings remain the beloved of God and the fall is part of the plan, bodily existence is painful and causes humanity to forget the love that binds it to God.

The servant is also Christ who also falls into a human body. This second sense of fall is what makes it possible for Christ to accompany Adam into the ditch of life and annul the separation from God symbolized by hell. In this way, Christ preserves the servant from endless death. When God creates humanity, its substance is knit to the Trinity. When Christ becomes incarnate, humanity's sensuality is knit into divine nature. Because of this double "one-ing," human nature and human suffering are both knit to the Trinity so that God is never alienated from humanity, neither the part that never falls nor the embodied, sinning, suffering part. Because human nature and human suffering are both welded to the divine nature through Christ, it would be impossible to perceive blame and sin in humanity. Christ shares human nature; to blame humanity would be tantamount to blaming Christ. All suffering and sin, all of the anguish of human history, is contained in this unity by which the divine nature is so united with human nature that nothing can happen to humanity that does not also happen to Christ. Humanity is loved by the Trinity just as Christ is loved by the Father.

This unity does not by itself explain why the fall into suffering was necessary. It is not just a "happy fault" because it produced such and so great a redeemer.[23] It is a happy fall because it serves an essential purpose in welding humanity into the deepest intimacy of divine love.

The servant has been sent on an errand to retrieve a treasure from the earth. Under the form of Christ, this is the hard labor of the cross. Humanity is the treasure the lord so urgently longs for. Redeemed humanity is the treasure that the servant, in the form of Christ, so joyously leaps away to obtain. The servant's joy alludes to Jesus' joy on the cross: "It is joy, bliss, and endless delight to me that ever I suffered the passion for thee; and if I could suffer more, I would suffer more."[24] But the servant has two meanings. In one sense, it is Christ, redeeming humanity from sin. But it is also humanity itself. Julian is less explicit about the treasure that humanity unearths for the lord. I will offer my own surmise, based on the logic of her text.

God "thirsts" for humanity. Like a mother longing for her child, like a lover longing for the beloved, the Trinity longs for humanity. God creates humanity already "one-ed" with the divine nature. But true love must also be returned. The Trinity is powerful, good, and wise, but reciprocal love cannot be created *ex nihilo*. Mechthild and Marguerite emphasized that love is possible only when it is freely given. Free will is necessary for genuine love, even if free will is also what makes sin possible. Sin and love are bound together by free will. Julian also thinks love must be freely given, but she sees it from a different angle.

Julian is looking at a world in which not only suffering but atrocity, catastrophe, and horror are the order of every day. To understand her context, we have to imagine a world in which Ebola erupts in waves over the course of our life and wipes out six out of every ten of our neighbors. Climate change creates devastating, unimaginable flooding; harvests become unpredictable, hunger stalks the land and famine causes massive starvation. Veterans and disenfranchised workers, mutilated by poverty and violence, become brigands that terrorize our cities and neighborhoods. Masses of poor are crushed by taxes and then by the savagery with which their protests are put down. To challenge the church, whose theologians and clerics oversee this regime, is to challenge the core of society: its critics are crushed with efficient brutality.

Julian is not worried about free will. She wants to know how this soul-mutilating evil could serve as an *essential* part of God's loving plan for humanity. In the exemplum she is shown, humanity falls into the ditch of history while it is retrieving a treasure greatly desired by God. What is this treasure and why is the evil of human experience the means for unearthing it? Or put another way, why can the love so treasured by the Trinity be perfected only through the outrages of sin and suffering?

Suffering can crush and destroy the human spirit, extracting from us our worse behavior. But, paradoxically, it is through suffering that profound compassion is born. The illness and wounds Julian prayed for at the beginning of her book open her to divine compassion. Suffering can destroy us, but it can also carve out a depth in which beauty, compassion, and intimate love are born. Our capacity for love must pass through the travails of suffering just as a child comes to adulthood only through the difficulties of gradual formation of their spiritual capacities.[25]

Love must be something that we choose and desire, that we seek and which forms in us over time. We might think of enduring marriages. Two young people, even if they love each other at the beginning, must learn how to love each other in the every-dayness of life, during disagreements, catastrophes, and the dissolution of youthful exuberance. The ripening of love from infatuation into the abiding tenderness and understanding of aging lovers requires time and commitment. The deepest qualities of enduring love are not born in an instant.

In Julian's vision, the Trinity recognizes that though suffering causes sin, it is only through suffering that the depths of love will be born. This treasure in the earth must be obtained by the servant; it cannot be created by God. But because Christ has united with human nature, the Trinity has made sure that humanity will succeed. It is *necessary* to learn to love God through suffering, but it is *possible* because Christ is with us. We cannot see it in our dark ditch, but sin and suffering are directed toward a single end. The Trinity has compassion for our hard labor but sees it in light of the beautiful treasure that is being unearthed. Because even sin has been built into creation as the occasion of our soul-making, there is no shame or blame in it.

In Julian's vision, while the servant languishes in the ditch, the lord dwells in a barren land. "And his sitting on the bare ground and desert means this: he made humanity's soul to be his own city and his dwelling place (which is the most pleasing of all of his works) and when humanity fell into sorrow and pain, it was not fit to serve in that noble position and so our kind Father, rather than give himself another place, sits upon the earth . . . until his dearworthy son had brought his city back to its noble beauty."[26] The Holy Trinity created humanity for its own dwelling place. Through exile and suffering this dwelling will become infinitely richer and more beautiful than it would otherwise be. God sees human evil and suffering, even at their most grotesque and destructive, in light of the arc of cosmic time. There is no wrath, no blame. There is an eternity of joy that will be accomplished by this sojourn in the ditch. Because we do not recognize this, our suffering is greatly intensified. Julian understands the showings she received as news to us in our exile. If we understood our individual stories in light of this grand narrative, our pain would be assuaged. Knowing how tenderly God loves us even at our worst and that there is a plan to transform our own and all humanity's suffering and evil into joy, we will be able to await our reconciliation "gladly and merrily without unreasonable sadness and useless sorrow."[27]

Suffering as the School for Compassion

In womanist, feminist, and other contemporary theology, there has been a strong criticism of the valorization of suffering in Christianity, the view that we must suffer to gain God's love or purge ourselves from sin. These criticisms should be taken very seriously. But the need to interpret how suffering can be theologically understood continues to be important; it is something we can neither definitively answer nor ignore. Julian is not saying that we should suffer because Christ suffers but that Christ suffers because we suffer. Because Christ has been woven into human nature, God is able to use suffering to expand our capacities for love and compassion. It is not empirically true that those who suffer much are more compassionate, though they can be. Sometimes the reverse is true. Julian is not making an empirical point but arguing that there is a much broader horizon of time; the darkness of human history is only one, relatively brief, moment of it. Unfortunately, it is all we see so the evils we experience can be overwhelming. But on the much larger time frame of eternity, sin and suffering will prove to be the very things that enlarged our soul to be capacious enough to provide a dwelling place for divine goodness. This may or may not be very satisfying, but it is her way of seeing in a desperate historical moment the efficacy of divine wisdom, compassion, and power.

By retelling the story of the fall and its redemption in a way that even sin plays a crucial role in the economy of salvation, the brutality of history is given a new meaning. As unlikely as it had seemed, Julian is able to imagine that God desires and is able to "make all things well." In this light, the depth of divine love is displayed with a rare intensity. The next two chapters will let us encounter the vividness of this love as it radiates from two of her central images: the motherhood of Christ and the wounded face of Christ.

13

Mother, Father, Spouse

Julian and the Holy Trinity

"And so I saw that God rejoices that he is our Father and God rejoices that he is our Mother and God rejoices that he is our very spouse and our soul his loved wife."[1]

For Julian, the great problem is how to comport herself in a world so suffused with suffering and evil. While it seemed obvious to many people in her time that God's anger could be discerned in the disasters that befell them, she insisted everything was a footprint of the Trinity's love and compassion.

Though she prayed for a deeper understanding of divine compassion as a young woman, what she was shown during her illness was much more unsettling than she anticipated.[2] It became difficult to reconcile the undiluted mercy of the Trinity with the realities of evil and with church teachings. But even before she fully understood what she saw, she seemed confident that, in some mysterious way, God has the desire and the power to "make all things well." Perhaps because of this insight into the suffering but persistent power of compassion, motherhood became for her a central image for God.

Mother Christ

One of the most moving things about Julian's theology, especially for contemporary women and men, is her emphasis on divine motherhood. She is not satisfied only to pair motherhood with fatherhood in a prayer or liturgy. She uses motherhood as a key to her theology of redemptive love.

Julian did not invent the metaphor of motherhood for God. It is a frequent image in the Bible where God is a mother in labor (Isaiah) or gently coaxing her child (Hosea) or a hen gathering her chicks under her wings (Matthew). "Can a woman forget her nursing child, or show no compassion for the child of her womb? Even these may forget, yet I will not forget you. See, I have inscribed you on the palms of my hands" (Isa. 49:15–16). The Hebrew word for womb is the root of the word for compassion. Anselm and other medieval monks sometimes used mother as an image for nurturing love.[3] His Holiness the Dalai Lama often uses motherhood as a model for compassion in his talks (which has been unsettling for some of my friends who did not have very compassionate mothers). But Julian is unusual in the systematic use to which she puts it.

The crucified face of Christ is the "fairest in heaven," but it is not the only face that Julian sees. Jesus, whose crucified face gives shape to her visions, is also for her the divine mother. We may get some sense of the particular meaning she gives to divine motherhood by noticing where it fits in the arc of her book.

Her book begins with the distressing vividness of Christ's death and the inexplicable assurance that "all will be well." As she encounters God's radical love and tenderness, her anxiety over its stark contrast with the church's teachings becomes unbearable. Finally, after fifty chapters of intensifying frustration, Jesus shows her an image of a lord and servant that turns the story of Christianity on its head. There is no anger, only love. There is no blame, only honor. After the sturm und drang of all of this, it is as if Julian is carried into a calm cove. Her book transitions from recounting the images she was shown to a more systematic presentation of a theology of compassion. Moving from image to theology, it is not lords and servants but mothers who provide the nearest analogy for God's creation and redemption of humanity. Like Mechthild and Marguerite, she required a feminine image to capture what it is that makes God so good, her power so enduring, and her wisdom so sublime. But instead of Lady Love, it is Mother Christ that is the cipher for the endlessly patient and effective force of divine compassion.[4]

When Julian systematically analyzes motherhood, she sees in Mother Christ's work a trinitarian structure. Motherhood is the ground of our making (one-ing), it is the taking of our nature (incarnation), and it is the action by which this grace spreads outward: "by the same grace of length and breadth and height and depth and all is one love."[5] The divine mother provides the initial impulse for our creation and remains devoted to us in mercy and grace when things become difficult. For Julian, what is most distinctive about divine love is that it is like a mother's desire that her children exist and thrive. Even before they are born, a mother loves her children and she continues to do so through all of the stages of their growing up. As Isaiah says human mothers might fail in their compassion, but the divine mother will never do this.

Mothers use various strategies to bring their children to maturity but they do not give up on them, even when they have made mistakes or gone astray. Where some might criticize mothers for seeing their children through rose-colored glasses, Julian sees this very feature as mirroring God's smiling affection for humanity. Whatever the ambiguities any of us might feel about our own mothers, for Julian, the great beauty of motherhood makes it a powerful icon of love. "The fair, lovely word, 'mother' is so sweet and so kind in itself that it may not truly be said of anyone but of him [Christ] and to him that is very mother of life and of all. To the properties of motherhood belongs kind love, wisdom, and knowing; and it is God."[6]

As Julian pursues the model of motherhood, she pays special attention to its physicality. In contrast to male theologians, we are invited by Julian to see in the materiality of women's bodies and in the insightfulness of their emotions the wisdom of God. Far from despising women's bodies, she delights in their particularity as revelations of the kind of love Christ has for us. Far from trivializing the wisdom of mothers, she identifies it as a mirror for divine wisdom. Physically and spiritually, Mother Christ labors, nurses, and holds humanity. As babies share their mother's body in the womb, Mother Christ shares her body with humanity in the incarnation, in the sacraments, and in the church. Julian argues for the fittingness of the maternal image because "the mother's service is nearest, readiest, and most certain: nearest because it is most kind; readiest because it is most loving; and most certain because it is truest."[7]

Christ's maternal care begins in creation, continues in the birth, nursing, and nurture of humanity. Just as a young woman may long to become pregnant, the idea of creation comes from Mother Christ. The Trinity is eternal, always fully and completely itself. But from this beginning-less eternity, Mother Christ animates the Trinity with a desire to create humanity. "When he [Christ] would, by full accord of all the Trinity, he made us all at once. And in our making he knit us and one-ed us to himself, by which one-ing we are kept as clean and noble as we were made. By the virtue of this precious one-ing we love our maker and delight in him, praise him and thank him and endlessly enjoy/rejoice in him."[8]

Julian uses birth as a complex metaphor for several elements of Christ's redemptive work. Creation is birthed by Mother Christ's desire for us. We are birthed a second time by Christ's desire for our salvation. Appropriately, it is by being birthed by a woman that Mother Christ becomes the mother of humanity. "Our kind mother, our gracious mother, because he would completely become our mother in all things, took the maiden's womb as the foundation of all of his own work."[9] Our eternal mother is born of a human mother and having shared the maternal nature in birth, Mother Christ gives birth in turn. This is hard labor of the passion, a labor that, like that of many mothers, ends in death. "Thus he sustains us within him in love, and labors until fullness of time so he would suffer the sharpest birth pangs and the most grievous pains that ever were or ever shall be, and died at the last."[10] But unlike human mothers, Mother Christ does not end in death and neither do her children: "We know that all our mothers bear us to pain and dying. Ah—what is that? But our true mother, Jesus, he alone bears us to joy and to endless living—blessed must he be!"[11] Mother Christ births us physically in creation and spiritually in redemption. "Thus in our true Mother, Jesus, our life, is grounded, in his own foreseeing wisdom from without beginning, with the high supreme goodness of the Holy Spirit. In the taking of our human nature he restored life to us, and in his blessed dying upon the cross, he birthed us into endless life."[12]

Mother Christ cares for us after we are born, teaching and nurturing her children. In caring for growing children, she "kindles understanding, directs our ways, eases conscience, comforts the soul, and lightens our heart . . . and he makes us love all that he loves for his love and to be well paid with him and with all his works."[13] In this pedagogical work, Mother Christ's tenderness is "without comparison."

Nursing provides another multidimensional metaphor for divine care. The physical nourishment a nursing mother gives to her child becomes, in Christ, food of salvation: "The mother may give her child suck from her milk. But our precious mother Jesus, he may feed us with himself and does so full courteously and tenderly with the blessed sacrament that is the precious food of very life." And just as an infant at the mother's breast is as peaceful and blissful as if there were no evil in the world, Mother Christ reveals the eternity of joy at her breast: "The mother may lay her child tenderly to her breast. But our tender mother Jesus, he may intimately lead us into his blessed breast by his sweet, open side, and show us therein part of the godhead and the joys of heaven with spiritual certainty of endless bliss."[14] This allusion to Jesus' wounded side refers back to her tenth showing in which Jesus looked into his blessed side and, rejoicing, said, "Lo how I loved you." In this showing, Jesus drew her attention to his wound and "showed a fair, delectable place, large enough for all humanity that shall be saved to rest in peace and in love."[15] We rest on the breast of Mother Christ as sweetly as a baby on her mother's breast. At the same time, this place of great intimacy is vast enough to hold all humanity.

Motherhood also symbolizes the great mercy the Trinity has for humanity through the tribulations that will bring it to maturity. A mother knows the needs of her child and protects her or him tenderly. As the child changes and has different needs, so the mother's methods change. As the child grows, she suffers it to be chastised so that it can receive the fullness of goodness and grace. But the child of Mother Christ's womb is never separated from her compassion. "We are brought back by the motherhood of mercy and grace into the womb of our human nature where we were created by the motherhood of natural love, which natural love never leaves us."[16] When evil befalls humanity, mercy and grace turn it to goodness and honor.

Julian argues that sin reveals the particular beauty of mercy. Just as an artist thirsts for a canvas on which to paint, the Trinity thirsts for humanity on which to lavish its mercy and grace. Mercy and grace are the properties within God that turn good against evil. This merciful work of bringing good from wickedness is the distinctive work of Jesus, our true mother. We have our beginning in the creativity of Mother Christ, and we can trust the gracious and merciful protection she ceaselessly lavishes upon us.[17] Mortal mothers may wish these things for their children, but the divine mother can accomplish them.

Julian's detailed discussion of the attributes of motherhood provide the key to understanding who God is. She desires children and loves them even before they are born. She is uniquely united with her children in the womb and, in contrast to human children, they are never separated from this "precious one-ing." In labor and self-sacrifice, she secures the birth of her child into existence and rebirth into spiritual maturity. She is tender with the child's suffering and merciful in its wrong-doing. She is not afraid to use discipline but never gives up on her child. She desires that all of her children flourish, and she cherishes them all with a relentless commitment to birth them into joy.

In working out her maternal theology, Julian continues to reflect on her theology of the fall. Mother Christ allows her children to fall because it is through this fall that humanity will be "strengthened by his sweet deed, then we willingly choose him, by his sweet grace, to be his servants and his lovers everlastingly without end." In an echo of the "happy fault," Julian indicates that part of the purpose of the fall is to reveal the intensity of God's love for us. The more severe the fall and grievous the suffering, the more we may blame ourselves. "But it is not so, because it is necessary for us to fall, and it is necessary for us to recognize it. For if we did not fall, we would not know how weak and miserable we are by ourselves—nor would we know so well the amazing love of our Creator." This willingness to use the fall for a greater good is rooted in Christ's maternal love: "The mother can allow the child to fall sometimes and to be distressed in various ways for its own benefit, but she can never permit any kind of peril to come to the child, because of her love. But even if our earthly mother could allow her child to perish, our heavenly Mother Jesus cannot allow us that are His children to perish."[18]

Julian's theology of motherhood reinforces the confidence that in making "all things well," all humanity will be saved. "By nature the child does not despair of the mother's love; by nature the child does not rely upon itself; by nature the child loves the mother and each one of them the other. . . . Thus I understood that all His blessed children who have been birthed from Him by nature shall be brought back into Him by grace."[19]

Julian does not contrast the tender love of the mother with the stern justice of a father. To the contrary, maternal love inflects the work of the whole Trinity. Mother Christ desired humanity and the Father and the Spirit joined in the work to bring this desire to fruition. They work as one, with one will and one desire. Nonetheless, it is Mother Christ who first desired us, who shares the greatest intimacy with us, and whose work is nearest to us in the labor of salvation.

The Holy Trinity

Maternal love provides the most comprehensive model for the kind of love God has for humanity, but it would be misleading to imply it is the only way Julian talks about divine love. As always, she thinks about love in a trinitarian way: "And thus in our making God almighty is our kindly Father, and God all wisdom is our kindly mother, with the love and the goodness of the Holy Ghost which is all one God, one lord. And in the knitting and the one-ing he is our very true spouse and we his loved wife and his fair maiden, with which wife he was never displeased. For he says: 'I love you and you love me and our love shall never be severed in two."[20]

Julian's understanding of the divine nature flows from the revelation given to her by "Jesus Christ, our endless bliss," but it is deeply trinitarian in its structure.[21] Some theologians use the Trinity to accommodate ethical contradictions: wrath and mercy, love and justice. But for Julian, the Trinity is united in its devotion and desire: power, love, goodness; majesty, wisdom, and goodness; Father, Son and Holy Ghost; Father, Mother, Spouse; truth, compassion, creativity. These triads evoke the synergistic efficacy of divine love. Who showed God's meaning? What was shown? Why was it shown?[22] Love, love, love. Three in one, one in three. A single essence dispersed, dancing through three personas.[23] Complementing divine motherhood, she also sees God as a courteous lord and a gracious spirit.

Divine Courtesy

As familiar, friendly, and intimate as we are with our Divine Mother, the Trinity is also majestic and awesome. But this majesty is not fearsome, it is courteous. By reinterpreting what a divine king might look like, she reenvisions the nature of power in light of the overarching themes of her work, especially the way it is related to sin.

The divine majesty has none of the arbitrary fierceness of nominalist or Reformation theology. Her use of the metaphor of "courtesy" to evoke divine goodness is drawn from feudalism, but as we have seen, the actual models she had for feudal power were not attractive ones. The secular and religious symbols of pomp and the opulence of privilege were jealously guarded. In alluding to the divine courtesy she is likening God to a feudal lord but imagining his relationship to his people in utterly different terms.

Julian is repeatedly struck by the "familiarity" or "friendliness" of the divine courtesy.[24] In contrast to human lords who jealously protect the markers of hierachy, the divine lord seeks to eliminate the barriers between humanity and divinity. In fact, the entire purpose of creation is precisely this. The lord does not need external signs of pomp to shore up his dignity or compel obedience. To the contrary, he clothes himself in most humble and vulnerable form and is born of a poor and lowly maiden. He exposes himself to humiliation and suffering. He uses the maternal wisdom of supposedly foolish and inferior women to illustrate something essential about divinity. He does not use coercion and violence to achieve his aim. Though he permits his beloved humanity to fall into the ditch of suffering and sin, he does not abandon it there. Where feudal justice would exploit the rawest forms of humiliation, mutilation, and death to restore its authority, the divine lord transforms blame into honor.

In seeing the copiously bleeding head of Christ, Julian perceives the juxtaposition of God's simultaneous familiarity and courtesy. "Our good lord, that is so reverent and fearsome is so intimate and courteous."[25] This friendliness brings her enormous joy. She imagines the unique happiness one would enjoy if a great lord were willing to be friendly with a lowly servant. Such a creature would think: "Lo what might this noble lord do more honorable and joyous to me than to show to me, that am so little, this marvelous intimacy? It is more joy and delight to me than if he gave me great gifts and were himself in a distant manner."[26]

In the parable of the lord and the servant, the lord is depicted sitting on the barren ground with no palace or dwelling place until humanity is restored. When this restoration is accomplished, all of the Trinity's labor is celebrated in a great feast where the lord, again, is near and intimate. He does not even take a great seat at the head of the hall but mingles among his friends like an attentive host, eager to make sure everyone is happy and enjoying themselves. "I saw our lord God as a lord in his own house, [where] he called all his dear-worthy friends to a solemn feast. He did not take a seat in his own house, but I saw him royally reign in his house and fill it with joy and mirth, himself endlessly gladdening and comforting his dear-worthy friends, most intimately and courteously, with marvelous melody of endless love, in his own fair, blessed face. Which glorious countenance of the godhead filled all heaven with joy and bliss."[27] Better than any gifts is the intimate love of this great lord, who gladdens his friends with feasting and music. For Julian, even the image of God as a sovereign or king becomes a name for the Trinity's intimate love for humanity.

Providential Goodness

The goodness of the trinitarian God is providentially present in everything, large and small. The Holy Spirit is especially associated with goodness and it is this goodness that infuses all of the divine works. This gives us grounds for hope and confidence, but when we turn our eyes from our meditations on this divine goodness to the realities of human history, we may find the transition jarring.

Julian describes seeing God "in a point." This is a quite different kind of image, one that balances the personal images of the divine mother or courteous lord. A point takes up no space or time and yet it is the center. Julian may have borrowed this image from Neo-platonic Christian theologians who liken God to a point from which everything radiates, though it is unclear whether Julian knew these writings.[28] The eternal Trinity is no place and no time but precisely in this way the divine goodness pervades all things. "I saw God in a point—that is to say, in my understanding by which sight I saw that he is in all things."[29]

While it is consoling to imagine this all-pervading goodness spreading through all of creation, it also implies that God must be present in evil and sin. "I beheld this with close attention, knowing in that sight that he does all that is done. I marveled in that sight with a soft dread and thought: [if that is true], what is sin?"[30] This troubles Julian because it is obvious to her that many things are quite alien to divine goodness. If God does all things, then why is there so much evil? And yet God insists that "all things are well done for our lord God does them all." God does not sin and yet uses sin as an element in the providential plan. For Julian, it is difficult to accept that God is the doer in all things. She is being compelled to accept that if God has the whole world in his hands, whatever happens is "God's will."

Really? The grotesque plague that killed more than half of the citizens of Norwich? The Lollards screaming as they died in fiery agony for criticizing the church's corruptions? The domestic violence, the infant mortality, a mother's grief? All of this was done by God? This is a standard theology of her time. God is so consumed with anger at human sin that no atrocity satisfies his justice. But Julian's showings indicate that this theology is completely wrongheaded. It is not anger and justice we see in history but love and courteous gentleness.

Through these showings, she is slowly and gradually brought to an understanding that makes this almost nauseating showing not only bearable but joyful. When we look at the horrors of history, it is shocking to imagine that God is the doer. In imposing this view on Julian, God's point is not that we accept everything as good, however cruel, because God did it. Rather, she is invited to see the sufferings of the world in the larger scheme in which all things are being drawn to a joyful conclusion. That joy can only be accomplished by going through the painful learning that comes to us through suffering. "I saw full certainly that he never changes his purpose in anything nor ever shall. . . . 'See, I am God. . . . I never leave my hand from my works nor ever shall. See I lead all things to the end that I ordained it to from beginning-less time, by the same might, wisdom, and love that I made it with. How should anything be amiss?'"[31] God's providence is universal, extending to all of creation everything that is made and loved by God.

The way Julian attempted to understand the atrocities of history in relationship to God's eternal will may not be entirely satisfying to many contemporary people. (I have myself been critical of theodicies like this one).[32] This kind of theodicy received its most devastating criticism in Dostoyevsky's novel *The Brothers Karamazov*. In the chapter titled "Rebellion," Ivan famously returned his ticket admitting him to paradise, if that paradise rested on the suffering of even one innocent child. He did not believe that an eternity of paradise could justify such suffering. Each of us will struggle with the painfulness of this question in our own ways. But Julian apparently found consolation in the belief that God could use even the worst of suffering to enhance the joy of humanity in an eschatological victory.

Through her complex images for God, Julian invites her readers to see all of human experience as part of the arc of salvation. It is the "thirst" of God to have all of humanity within Godself. "He continually draws and drinks and still He thirsts and yearns."[33] Everything in creation is designed to quench that thirst. When she says that God's plan will not be thwarted, she seems to mean that even the devastations of human sin cannot turn God aside from the desire for perfect intimacy with humanity. In this sense, her theodicy is entirely different from what might be more familiar in her time. We suffer the difficulties of history, but they do not testify to God's anger or violence. In a strange way, they remain under the auspices of divine compassion, whose will and desire cannot be turned aside. Like Julian, we may remain bewildered by suffering and find it difficult to reconcile experiences of sin and pain with divine love and compassion. But she insists that we can be confident in the tender wisdom of the Mother, the energizing goodness of the Spirit, and the efficacious power of the Father that the promise that "all will be well" is woven in from the beginning and will not be thwarted.

14

The Fairest Face in Heaven

Julian's Passion

> His blessed face, which is the fairest of heaven, the flower of earth, and the fruit of the maiden's womb. Then how might this image be so discolored and so far from fair?[1]

When I teach Julian's *Showings* to undergraduates, they are so put off by the grisly opening that they are often unable to pay attention to her remarkable theology. But for Julian, it is through wounds, trauma, and despair that we come to know the fullness of Mother Christ's love for humanity. But afflictive suffering is precisely what most of us absolutely do not want to look at. We avert our eyes or make it more palatable through theories that justify it. We glimpse veterans' wounds through a mist of patriotic jingles. We encounter children too hungry to succeed in school only as collateral damage, explained away by economic theories. The atrocities occurring in our prisons and detention centers are deflected by confidence that the guilty deserve to suffer. When the savagery of violence becomes unbearable, we change the channel. But if we are to understand Julian's theology, we must keep these concrete forms of suffering in mind. For her, the brutal and gruesome suffering of Christ is not an atonement to an angry Father but an icon of suffering humanity. These wounds haunt her and she cannot turn away.[2] But they are wounds that invite us into the universal and undivided compassion of God for the world.

"I Saw This Sight of Plenteous Bleeding"

One of the first things Julian sees as her visions unfold is a strange combination of horrible brutality and great joy:

> In this showing suddenly I saw the red blood trickling down from under the garland, hot and freshly and most plenteously, just as it was at the time of His Passion when the garland of thorns was pressed against his blessed head. . . . And in the same showing suddenly the Trinity almost filled my heart with joy and I understood it shall be like that in heaven without end. . . . For the Trinity . . . is our Maker, the Trinity is our Keeper, the Trinity is our everlasting Lover, the Trinity is our endless Joy and Bliss, through and in our Lord Jesus Christ.[3]

Although this is the very beginning of the revelations Julian will receive, it was essential to show her that the suffering she was witnessing was not only for humanity's salvation but for its joy.

Julian offers us news that the distortions of sin are not absolute and they do not overthrow God's love for humanity. But hers is news entering a war zone, and as in all war zones, truth is controlled by a propaganda machine. The showing given to her represents a systematic alternative to the theology by which her whole world is structured. She herself is caught in the maw of a propaganda machine dedicated to silencing what she has seen. The efficiency of that machine grinds on. Neither our society nor our theology take with real seriousness the possibility that "love was his meaning." The confidence that most of humanity is destined for endless suffering is a core belief shared by the vast majority of Christians. Perhaps the callousness this requires helps underwrite a general indifference to suffering. It provides a metaphysical background to divisions that structure our society between those deemed worthy of good things—medical care, respect, food, education, protection from police brutality—and those unworthy.

In our time as in hers, actions and beliefs, politics and theology intertwine. As we try to understand how Christ's bloody face is the "fairest in heaven," we need explore Julian's own struggle to accept what she has seen.

Denial and Betrayal

"But Peter said, 'Man, I do not know what you are talking about!' At that moment, while he was still speaking, the cock crowed. The Lord turned and looked at Peter. Then Peter remembered the word of the Lord, how he had said to him, 'Before the cock crows today, you will deny me three times.' And he went out and wept bitterly" (Luke 22:60–62).

When Julian describes her illness, she admits that her first response to what she was shown was to deny it. When she wakes up, she finds her pain has returned, and she tells a monk who has come to visit her that she has been "raving." Even as she writes this years later, she recognizes this as a betrayal of Jesus' gift to her and is filled with remorse.[4]

That night she is again visited with a vision, but this time it is not Jesus but the "fiend" that comes to her in the shape of a young man, terrifying and horrible, who attempts to strangle her. He is ugly and misshapen, "but with his paws he held me by the throat and would have strangled me but he was not able." Scarcely alive, she is awakened by "our courteous lord," and those around her bathe her temples with water.[5] Jesus returns once more, saying, "full sweetly: Know it now well, it was not madness ['no raving'] that you saw today. But take it and believe it, and keep it within you and comfort yourself with it and trust it and you shall not be overcome."[6] In this short scene, Julian's theodicy is played out in miniature. Julian is threatened by evil and succumbs to the temptation to betray Christ. Realizing what she has done, she is ashamed, but Jesus shows no wrath, only tenderness.

To clarify this chronology: as a young woman, Julian prays for an illness that will intensify her experience of divine compassion. In her thirties, she experiences just such a mortal illness and is shown a long revelation of divine love. She awakens and says to a visiting friend that she had been delirious. This moment of weakness provides an opening to the devil who chokes her and attempts to silence her.[7] She is saved when Christ returns and reminds her of everything she was shown by him. She was not delirious, and if she stands by what she was shown she will never be overcome.

When Satan attacks her, Christ helps to fend him off but insists that she will only be free of these temptations if she remains faithful to the revelation he gave her. This she finds almost impossible to do. She enters the anchorhold and writes down a brief account of what happened, leaving out key parts. This first text is "A Vision Showed to a Devout Woman," often called simply the "Short Text." Fifteen years later, Jesus returns to her and gives her an inner teaching. It is a summary of what she had been told many times and in many ways in the original showing but somehow it seems to move into her more deeply. She uses it as the conclusion of her later text "Revelation of Divine Love," often called either *Showings* or the "Long Text": "Love is my meaning. . . . Hold you onto this and you will know more of the same. But you will never know anything other without end."[8] But even at this point, she is not able to acquiesce to the full consistency and power of what she is being taught.

Another five years pass, some twenty years after the original showing, and she receives another inner teaching that seems finally to unlock the truth for her. It takes decades before she finds the wherewithal to write down "his meaning." In writing down the mature theology of her Long Text, it may not be that she understood for the first time but that she finally found the courage to accept what she was being taught. What was this truth that she had to struggle so hard to accept?

"The Fiend . . . Held Me by the Throat"

As Jesus and the fiend contend for her, we witness a symbolic display of how compelling a theology of violence can be. Who is this "fiend" who tries to strangle her into silence—and seems almost to succeed? "Our good lord showed the enmity of the fiend, whereby I understood that all that is contrary to love and peace is of the fiend and of his party."[9] By contrast, sin, as Porete also argued, is precisely ignorance of divine love. It is this "unknowing [of love] that most hinders God's lovers."[10]

Jesus tells her over and over and over that God is love, that God loves all of humanity, that the desire and wisdom of God are eternal and never change in their purpose. She is shown the meaning of the incarnation and passion. It is not a blood atonement. It does not turn aside God's anger. There is no such thing. Christ becomes incarnate in order to knit human nature to the divine nature. He suffered on the cross to overcome the "fiend" whose lies and violence block our knowledge of God's love. There is no wrath and there is no sin. These are lies relentlessly spewed out by the "fiend's" propaganda machine to disguise from us who we are and who God is.

Julian's theology is running headlong against crucial elements of medieval theology. In earlier centuries, the passion was understood to manifest the love the Trinity had for humanity. Evil was personified by the devil, and its intransigence was symbolized by images of bondage or slavery. The Trinity conspired together and devised a plan to disempower evil by disguising itself in human form. Jesus' death ransomed humanity from bondage to the devil, manifesting the love of the Father, Son, and Spirit. During the Middle Ages, sin was understood to be not only bondage but also guilt. Every human being from the time of its conception deserved endless torment in hell. The idea that the Trinity, through Christ, ransomed humanity from the bondage to evil and the devil was replaced by the idea that the divine Father required a bloodletting before he would let humanity escape his wrath, but he allowed the death of his divine son, Jesus, to satisfy this bloodlust. Because of this death, some part of humanity would be permitted to avoid the punishment it deserved. This relocates to the Father the wrath and violence once attributed to Satan. In this theological sleight of hand, the leering face of the devil has replaced the "fairest in heaven." It is as if Aslan did not have to save Edmund from the White Witch of Narnia but from God.[11]

By contrast, Julian is shown that there is no anger and no fault; the passion is the work of the whole Trinity to reintegrate beloved humanity more fully into the divine life. Julian can neither accept nor reject the love that was revealed to her. She recognizes the teachings of the church are completely at odds with what she has been shown. The conflict is not that God's mercy and love allow some portion of humanity to be saved. That is church doctrine. But in seeing that there is no wrath or blame, she is shown a more radical love. This unconditional love, this thirsting of God for humanity undercuts the whole system of church doctrine and practice. If she accepts her inward teachings, it seems she must renounce her faithfulness to the church, which is unbearable to her.

> "Good lord, I see that you are very truth and I know surely that we sin grievously all day and are very blameworthy. And I may neither leave the knowing of this nor do I see in this showing any manner of blame. How may this be? For I knew the common teaching of the holy church and by my own feeling that the blame of our sins hangs on us continually from the first man until we come to heaven. Then this miracle, that I saw our lord God showing us no more blame then if we were as clean and as holy as the angels in heaven. And between these two contraries my reason was greatly afflicted by my blindness and could have no rest."[12]

Julian is feeling with particular intensity the pain that many religious people feel when the church's teachings or practices are inferior to the deepest wisdom and goodness to which the church is meant to bear witness. The church is a gift of divine love that, like humanity itself, is loved and cherished by God. It is a mother's breast at which we find comfort. But it does not escape the human condition. The very institutions intended to mediate divine love are themselves forgetful of its amazing and unbelievable goodness. The church is itself in the ditch along with humanity, sharing its confusions. This is the cruel irony that Christ's lovers suffer when the "fiend" conquers. In Julian's vision, the devil attempts to strangle and silence her. In her time, the church was teaching a theology of violence, strangling and silencing those who would challenge it.

"Where Now Is the Point of Your Grief?"

Julian's is a "revelation of love."[13] She is shown the passion in grizzly detail in order to be shown that "his meaning" is, and always was and will be, love. To convey this love, Christ introduces her to an interpretation of the cross that is entirely different from the one that would be familiar to her.

The first ten of Julian's sixteen showings detail Jesus' slow death on the cross: the crowning with thorns, the discoloring of his face, his scourging, his last pains and cruel dying. But in the midst of this terrible anguish, Julian records an astonishing exchange: Jesus suddenly asks her if she feels well paid [satisfied] in all that he suffered. She is a little overwhelmed: "Yes, good lord, gramercy [thanks be!]. Yes, good lord, blessed may you be!" Jesus responds to her in all sweetness: "If you are well paid then I am well paid. It is a joy, a bliss, and endless delight that I suffered passion for you."[14]

When Christ is at the uttermost point of death his visage suddenly changes and he is filled with "blissful cheer" that fills Julian with joy. He asks her, somewhat slyly: "Where now is the point of your pain and grief?"[15] Christ almost mischievously shows Julian that what she is seeing is actually the human condition and that the agony of the human experience will just as quickly turn to joy. "I understood that we be now, in our lord's meaning, on his cross with him in our pains and in our suffering, dying . . . [and] suddenly he shall change his appearance to us and we shall be with him in heaven . . . and then shall all be brought to joy."[16]

The courage that allowed her to witness suffering allows her also to see that "we are his bliss, we are his noble gift, we are his honor, we are his crown."[17] Jesus wants Julian to participate in the joyousness of the divine life. Compassion for humanity brings this life near to us and compassion for Jesus turned out to be what brought Julian near to the joyousness of that life. Jesus wanted her to see the eschatological horizon in which all would be well. But perhaps even more, he wanted her to see that love does not blame and condemn; it delights in us, even in our frailty. The passion was not a dour sacrifice but the Trinity's plan for drawing humanity into the heart of God through the door of compassion. Her conversations with Christ were quite "merry." There is no self-flagellation about how our sins required so much suffering on our behalf. For Julian, the wounds of Christ are the doorway to the infinite gentleness of divine compassion.

"Thus I saw how Christ has compassion on us because of sin. And just as I had been filled with the compassion for Christ's passion, likewise I was now filled with compassion for all of my fellow Christians."[18] Compassion cleaves open our heart so that we can pour ourselves out in sympathy for the entire human race. In and through Christ, we touch suffering with tenderness and compassion. The hopeless misery of the ditch of suffering is transformed into paradise. The husk of our individual humanity falls away, and we are naked to the divine life flowing through all of creation.

The violent images of the passion with which Julian opens her book seem an incongruous opening to this story of delight and merriment, intimacy and bliss. She walked the streets of Norwich watching hideous mounds of rotting plague victims pile up, the maimed and lame veterans wander the streets, and the famine survivors starve; she witnessed the casual brutality of the church and of brigands, court executioners, and enraged serfs. Through the gift of divine compassion, Julian recognized in all of these faces, disfigured by rage and grief, the glimmering of the "fairest face in heaven."

He Showed a Fair, Delectable Place Large Enough for All Humanity[19]

Suffering cleaves us open to divine love and prepares us to be the dwelling place of God. This work is endless joy for the Trinity, and through this work it will become humanity's joy as well. But this reorientation of suffering from punishment and guilt to something held and cherished by the divine love was only one element of the revelation that was so difficult for her to accept. After all, accepting that "those who are saved" are saved by Christ's wounds is hardly a violation of church doctrine.

If all is to be well, as she is promised, it cannot be in a sentimental, avert your eyes from what is really happening sense. All will be well when the atrocity of *human* suffering is transformed: that is, it is not a particular suffering or my suffering or the suffering of parts of the human race that I care about (or imagine God cares about)—it is *human* suffering. It is not this or that person that falls into the ditch, it is humanity; for in God's sight all humanity is one person and one person is all humanity.[20] Neither is it the case that some sin is shown to be shameful and unforgivable and others are shriven. Sin itself is shown to have no existence. Sin is necessary, it is the method by which the union between humanity and divinity will be accomplished. For that reason, there is no shame or blame in it.

"Let no man or woman take this just for himself, for it is not so: it is general [universal]. For it was for our precious mother Christ that this fair human nature was made, for the honor and the nobility of human creation, and for the joy and bliss of human salvation, just as he saw, knew, and recognized from without beginning."[21] The entire logic of what Julian was shown indicates that if any suffering remains, if any blame or shame is unhealed, then Christ's wounds remain open and God's thirst remains unquenched.

Compassion is the doorway for understanding who God is. This seems to be very consoling to readers and interpreters of Julian who enjoy reading her beautiful emphasis on love. But this compassion opens Christianity to a revelation of the undivided love the Trinity has for *humanity* in a way that shatters the duality between saved and damned that some consider essential to its worldview. The idea that God truly loves *the world* can be intolerable, even for those who most admire her.[22] But she is given to understand that it is precisely the whole world that is held in God's hand: "it lasts and ever shall for God loves it. And so shall all things be by the love of God."[23]

Whatever is "contrary to love and peace" is in the parliament of the devil and his party. If we worship a torturer, we worship the fiend.

The Fiend Is Overcome

In Julian's vision, she sees blood flowing so copiously from Christ that she wonders how the bed and the whole room are not soaked in it. As she beholds this, words are formed in her soul: "Herewith is the fiend overcome."[24] She sees the devil's great malice but she sees also his "unmight:" his powerlessness. Like Mephistopheles in Goethe's *Faust*, Julian's fiend is frustrated because all the evil he *would* do is thwarted by God and all the evil he *does* do serves only to increase humanity's joy in the end. In seeing this, Julian laughs at the sheer joy of seeing what seems on earth so all-powerful and so malicious turned to nothing. The evil that rules the world with terror and brutality is revealed in its true form: "unmight" and nothingness. This unmasking of evil shows the intransigence of injustice and our seeming impotence against regimes of power from the divine perspective.

But this unmasking alone is not enough. We human beings are enmeshed in power structures that shape us, precede us, and entangle even our good intentions with destructive consequences. It is not enough to open the prison gates and let us stumble into the light. We have been in prison so long we do not know any other reality and do not know how to function in the light. We do not know how to integrate the luminous goodness of the divine image with the concrete and fragile flesh that embodies it.

The passion must therefore not only defeat an external devil, it must also heal what has been maimed by the great deception that obscures Mother God's love. This is why the mode of Julian's writings are revelatory "showings." Where Marguerite emphasized the path of mystical unknowing as the path toward unity with divine goodness, for Julian, the path is preeminently one of seeing and understanding. The fundamental cause of all suffering and sin is precisely the failure to grasp that God loves us.

This is why the visual center of Julian's showings is the grisly ugliness of Christ's death. In one sense, the Trinity does not recognize that human nature has ever fallen away. "Knit and one-ed" with God, we are eternally held in the safety of the divine womb. But the mutilation of the human spirit is quite real. The grotesqueness of Jesus' death mirrors to us our true state. This intense visual image of affliction does not display the horror of disobedience or the shamefulness of our cruelty. It shows to us the mutilation of the spirit by the "works of the fiend," that is, by our inability to dwell in the knowledge of love. This is the terrible fissure in our nature.

The misshapen ugliness of Christ's face is the visual representation of sin. Sin is "unknowing" of God's love. Believing God is wrathful and our sin is too shameful causes religious people doubt and despair. But we do not reject our despair over God's goodness as a sin, because we do not recognize it as such. To the contrary, we believe it to be a spiritual virtue.[25] Christ appears in such a terrible form to show us what sin looks like: that is, not only the great human evils that haunt every byway but also the spiritual dismemberment—by religion—of the knowledge of God's love.

Julian ends her book with the recognition that her book was begun with God's grace but it had not yet been performed. It is not possible to be a member of the human race and not participate in the mixed messages we receive from religion and society. Even if we renounce the violent theologies we learned in church or theology class, some shadow of a stern sky-father infiltrates our mind, telling us that domination is the order of things and that no human being is really worthy of love. Even if we reject the belief that certain races are inferior than others or that women have fewer rights over their bodies than men do or that nature is a resource for our greed, these ideas remain in the social atmosphere. But as Mechthild also insisted, Lady Love continues to send us messengers, news in our exile that even now humanity is adored and cherished. We are invited to participate in that love and to radiate it back to the world.

Holy Thirst

That Julian struggled so long to accept what she saw shows how deeply our "unknowing" of divine love penetrates even the most beautiful spirit. That Marguerite was so horrifically murdered for witnessing to this love shows how important it is to governments and churches to conceal it. But Julian insisted the "fiend" has been overcome, and she laughs in delight to see it.[26] We do not see this and so suffer from the sin and suffering inherent in the human condition, and we suffer the mutilation of our spirit by our "unknowing" of love. But she is confident that we will all see for ourselves the unity of love that has held us all from the dawn of eternity. "We shall all say with one voice: 'Lord, blessed must thou be, for it is thus, it is well."[27] All will be well, and every manner of thing will be well, and we will all see it. In the meantime, the Trinity sits in a barren land waiting for us. God thirsts for all humanity. Until *all* are reconciled, still God "thirsts and longs."[28]

Let us renounce the works of the "fiend." Let us thirst and long. Let us find the courage to believe that all humanity is "knit and one-ed" with God. May we believe that nothing can deter God's eternal desire for us. In our compassion for another, for all others, the joy of this desire will continually be reborn into this world.

Conclusion

Delivered from Captivity

Contemplative Women in the Twenty-First Century

> As the only movement in medieval monastic history that was created by women and for women—and not affiliated with, or supervised by, a male order—beguines bear many of the characteristics . . . associated with religious communities dominated by women: a lack of overarching governmental structures, a low level of internal hierarchy, a tendency toward the sacralization of routine work, the use of dance and ecstasy in worship. . . . It is then . . . by creating and sustaining for seven centuries this unique and supportive environment for single women of all ages, ranks, and intellectual ambitions, that beguines made their most important contribution to religious and social life.[1]

Our journey through the lives and works of three great-hearted, God-intoxicated medieval women brings us back to our own time with liberating news of divine love and goodness. All three were familiar with difficulty, and yet they sing to us of joy. We read them now not out of vague historical curiosity but because they can inspire our own spiritual journeys and theological formation. What would this erotic, compassionate Christianity look like today? Each of us, like these women themselves, will discover that for ourselves. I will close with a few of my own reflections.

"Set the Point of Our Thought on This Blissful Beholding."[2]

These women invite us to rediscover contemplative practice as part of Christian faith. The modern period and its emphasis on belief has obscured how important meditation has been to Christianity. Whether one takes up meditation or not, it is an impoverishment of our understanding of faith to think of it only as believing things. Contemplative practices can help awaken our hearts to the nearness of divine love and make it more natural to radiate this love to others.

There are many ways contemporary Christians are exploring contemplative practices. Centering prayer groups proliferate. Church sponsored quiet days during Lent or Advent provide a pause during hectic seasons. Taize services are becoming more common. Retreats are available for groups or individuals. Some churches are recovering the ancient practice of lectio divina. This is a spiritual reading of Scripture that bypasses historical criticism and moralistic literalism alike to encounter the living Spirit in our own lives. Meditation teachers can provide guidance in practices of focusing the mind and opening it to the divine presence. Contemplative practice might be something as simple as using gardening or evening walks as a time for quiet and mindful attention to the world's beauty. Art, journaling, collaging, poetry, and dance are other ways to connect to our hearts in more vivid and refreshing ways.

Contemplative practices can be helpful because they provide more access to those parts of the human spirit that we pay less attention to. From a contemplative point of view, the heart is the place where the soul opens to God and silently enters into communion. This intimacy can uncover old wounds that need healing and bring light to unlit rooms. The heart is an organ of compassion and joy. Finding ways to connect to God present within enlivens us to the beauty and goodness all around.

Community

Reading these women invites us to think about different ways of being in community and finding communities that nourish us. They all remained part of the body of Christ and were nourished by the church's sacraments and traditions. But they also needed more than what clerics could provide. They all seemed to be in conversation with other likeminded women and men, reading and writing for a small circle of Christians who wanted to deepen their devotion through regular practices.

Women and men today also create community at the edges of the church. I have been part of a wild and wonderful group of women that meets once a year to do art, walk, talk, eat, sing, and share our journeys. Another group of women I have been a part of has met to "wander home" together: praying, worshiping, crying, and dancing together. A retreat with a local congregation of Presbyterian women brought together women of all ages to meditate and pray, walk and hike, play and imbibe together. These small, temporary communities find a depth of collective wisdom to hold the loss of children, of faith, of innocence and to hold with equal agility the simple joy of being together, doing yoga, or creating new forms of worship. Not governed by a liturgical structure or traditional theologies, we let the spirit move us and hold us in creative and life-giving ways.

I am also part of a more spread out community of people who are committed to a pattern of regular individual silent retreats at a small house of prayer in the middle of nowhere, Georgia. Without a word, we smile and nod as we pass the vegetables around the table or pass as we walk in the meadow. Somehow this silent communion binds us together, and we are all held by the quiet intensity of prayer.

However it happens—in weekly prayer groups, in the temporary intimacy of a single retreat, in the silence of a contemplative community—finding community and communion nourishes the spiritual journey and awakens us to the creativity of this path.

Dark Night

These women also teach us that the faith journey wanders off the clearly marked trail and renounces the security that comes from familiar beliefs. "The deeper I sink, the sweeter I drink," Mechthild sings;[3] but this sinking requires the courage to identify ways in which we are clinging to the needs of our ego rather than seeking God with all the energy of our desire. Egocentrism takes many forms in the religious life. Julian gently uncovers the way we project onto God our own anger and condemnation. Our very faithfulness condemns us to despair when we are unable to turn to the goodness and love of the Divine Mother in perfect trust. Marguerite encourages us to cast off images that have become substitutes for God. It takes a lot of courage to work with mind and heart to unearth our subtle fears and attachments.

Beverly Lanzetta points out that women and others marginalized by the church have a particular kind of "dark night."[4] If we have internalized religiously based homophobia, patriarchy, or racism, then coming to a deeper awareness of divine love will mean undoing the damage done by religion itself.

Cynthia Bourgeault trained with Father Thomas Keating, who helped found the centering prayer movement. She describes ways in which centering prayer can help unearth destructive mental patterns. "In my own practice of this prayer, I have learned by repeated experience that the 'reward' for a period of committed sitting is often the emergence of a patch of pain long buried and several days of emotional turmoil."[5] But Bourgeault goes on to describe the power of unitive consciousness that emerges from this practice.

Like Lanzetta, she finds women's wisdom to be a powerful resource. Working with the figure of Mary Magdalene, she argues that this "mysterious, alchemical feminine was kept alive. Until at last, in our own times, it comes above ground again, asking us to awaken yet again to the morning of resurrection and find ourselves in the garden, awaiting the encounter that can change our institutional hearts."[6]

The Wound of Compassion, the Wound of Longing[7]

The wisdom of these women reminds us that desire and compassion, love of God, and juicy, joyous love for humanity flow together. Many Christians hunger for justice in this difficult world but sometimes forget that there can be a sweetness to our longing. We long for God and we long for good things to come to others—all others—in the same way we might long for a letter from a distant beloved. The distance between us is like a wound, but the desire that connects us is sweet.

We are not likely to arrive at a historical moment when injustice, poverty, and oppression are wiped away. But in our longing and our compassion we bring the goodness of the risen Christ into the present moment. Longing makes what is distant near, and compassion fills the darkest hour with divine light. As Cynthia Bourgeault argues, Jesus is "*present*: alive, palpable, vibrantly connected . . . the walls between realms are paper thin. . . . The kingdom of heaven is not later, it is *lighter*: it exists right here. . . . God is not only for us, but *with* us."[8]

What does it mean to believe in God? Not only myths and images but in divine reality? We learn from these women that what appears rests on what does not appear. Christ's nearness shows us that the ugliness of suffering conceals the "fairest face in the world." The practical world of getting and spending is undergirded by the sheer, useless beauty of a cosmos that rests in divine love. We can live as if war and poverty, as if work or stale relationships, defined us and our world. Or we can live as if beauty and love are the most real things in the world. We do not have to do that; but if we do, then our lives will be more joyful and compassionate.

The wisdom of these women—ancient and contemporary—is that we can be free. The captivities that bind us—emotional, spiritual, institutional—can be relinquished. We are called to sweetness. We are called to joy. This is the countercultural wisdom contemplative women offer to Christianity and to the world.

Notes

Short references are provided in the notes. Readers interested in full bibliographical data or who wish to pursue further research are encouraged to consult the bibliography, where full publication data is provided for all sources in the notes.

Introduction

1. Marguerite Porete, *Mirror of Simple Souls*, chap. 122.
2. Teresa of Avila, *The Interior Castle*, First Mansion, chap. 1, p. 29.
3. *Mirror of Simple Souls*, chap. 31.
4. Ibid.
5. Julian of Norwich, *Revelations*, chap. 75.
6. Athanasius, *On the Incarnation*.
7. Bernard McGinn is a good interpreter of this movement; see, for example, *Varieties of Vernacular Mysticism*.
8. Emily Holmes and Wendy Farley, *Women, Writing, Theology: Transforming a History of Exclusion* is a fine reflection on the physical and psychological violence that has excluded women writers from the theological tradition. It also recovers the voices of many of these lost women. (It may seem self-serving of me to mention this book, as I am listed as a coeditor, but that should not discredit the fact that the women gathered to write the chapters of this book are excellent and important thinkers).
9. My partner, a graduate student in church history in the 1990's, was told she could not do research on Marguerite Porete if she expected to get a job because Marguerite was a "heretic."
10. Frank Tobin, introduction to *Flowing Light of the Godhead*, 13.
11. Introduction to *Mirror of Simple Souls*, translated and introduced by Ellen Babinsky, 19.
12. Walter Simons notes that the punishment of having their tongues cut out was applied to women "because their crime was defined as one of speech." *Cities of Ladies*, 12.

13. "The Monetary Fluctuations in Philip IV's Kingdom of France and Their Relevance to the Arrest of the Templars," Ignacio de la Torre and "Terror, Torture and the Truth, Testimonies of the Templars Revisited," Thomas Kramer, both in *The Debate on the Trial of the Templars*, edited by Jochen Burgtore et al. provide much detail in the unfolding of this narrative.
14. He refers to the Paris scholastic Henry of Ghent, who argues that women cannot be doctors of theology because they lack the marks of doctoral status: constancy, efficacy, authority, and effect. They may teach approved doctrine in private, in "silence," and to women but cannot teach to men because it is dishonorable to men and incites them to lust. Bernard McGinn, introduction to *Meister Eckhart and the Beguines in the Context of Vernacular Theology*, p. 1.
15. Joseph Kelly's review of *Literature and Heresy in the Age of Chaucer* by Andrew Cole draws attention to these mechanisms as an English version of the "invention of heresy" and the "invention of lollardism."
16. Introduction to *Mirror of Simple Souls*, translated and introduced by Ellen Babinsky, p. 17.
17. Introduction to *Mirror of Simple Souls*, translated by Edmund Colledge, J. C. Marler, and Judith Grant, lxxvi.
18. Amy Hollywood, "Suffering Transformed: Marguerite Porete, Meister Eckhart, and the Problem of Women's Spirituality," *Meister Eckhart and the Beguines in the Context of Vernacular Theology*, ed. Bernard McGinn, 108.
19. Ellen Babinsky uses these terms to describe Marguerite in her introduction of *Mirror of Simple Souls*, 21.
20. From *The Acts of the Christian Martyrs*, texts and translation by Herbert Musurillo, available various places, including http://www.pbs.org/wgbh/pages/frontline/shows/religion/maps/primary/perpetua.html.
21. "The Trial of Marguerite Porete (1310)." The chronicler William of Nangis describes the trial and execution of Marguerite Porete, 1310, translated by Richard Barton and available at www.uncg.edu/~rebarton/margporete.htm.
22. Teresa of Avila, *The Interior Castle*, First Mansion, chap. 1, 28–29.

Prologue

1. Walter Simons, *City of Ladies*, 140.
2. There are several books that provide a rich picture of beguine life. One of the best and most straightforward is *Brides in the Desert* by Saskia Murk-Jansen. Another excellent source is *Cities of Ladies: Beguine Communities of the Medieval Low Countries 1200–1565* by Walter Simons.

Chapter 1: "Serve Nobly, . . . and Fear Nothing Else"

1. Hadewijch, Letter 2.86, *Complete Works*.
2. Saskia Murk-Jansen, *Brides in the Desert: The Spirituality of the Beguines*, 27.
3. We do not know what Mary herself thought. Beatrice of Nazareth's biography also shows similar preoccupations, though they do not appear in Beatrice's own writings.
4. Among many good books on medieval women's spirituality are those by Carol Walker Bynum, including her ground-breaking work *Holy Feast, Holy Fast*. More recent scholarship refines her analyses, but this remains a fine work.
5. Richard Valentasis and Peter Brown are among many recent reappraisers of asceticism. Cynthia Bourgeault's discussion of the "imaginal" realm in *The Meaning of Mary Magdalene* also provides insight into this area.
6. Beatrice was herself a Cistercian nun, but her writings were known to the beguines and seemed to influence Marguerite Porete's theology.

7. Suzanne Kocher identifies influences more particularly to include Cistercian abbot Gerard of Liege and an anonymous Dominican nun as influences, particularly on Marguerite Porete. *Allegories of Love in Marguerite Porete's* Mirror of Simple Souls, 64, 69.
8. Love songs to God never go entirely out of favor. Sweet Honey and the Rock still sing "Feel Something Drawing Me On." "Can't Nobody Love Me Like Jesus" is still recorded and was sung recently at a vigil for someone on death row. Congregations still sing of Jesus' tender calling in the hymn "Softly and Tenderly Jesus Is Calling" by Will L. Thompson.
9. Anticipating the more well-known *Exercises of Saint Ignatius*, twelfth century monks such as Guigo II (*Ladder of the Monks*) and Aelred of Rievaulx (*Treatises and Pastoral Prayer*) offer detailed instructions for entering into biblical narratives as a way to reform mental habits and prepare the soul for love. *Lectio divina* remains a popular practice. There are many books describing this in modern terms, including a classic of the contemplative renewal of contemplative practices, Basil Pennington's Lectio Divina*: Renewing the Ancient Practice of Praying with Scripture*.
10. Robin Anne O'Sullivan, "The School of Love: Marguerite Porete's *Mirror of Simple Souls*," *Journal of Medieval History*, 149.
11. Ibid., 154.
12. The use of religious rhetoric to justify opposite moral attitudes toward men and women has not disappeared in the modern world. We still hear rape excused by supposedly loose behavior or revealing clothing of its victims. We read of the harshness suffered by pregnant or "loose" women in the Magdalene laundries, which closed as recently as 1996. As recently as last week's newspaper we continue to read of the protection priests receive from the Vatican after their sexual abuse has come to light. Religious and political parties rife with sexual indiscretion still deploy their moral capital to make sure women do not have access to birth control, pre- or postnatal health care, or decisions about their pregnancies.
13. Gilbert of Tournai, *Collectio de scandalis ecclesiae*, ed. P. A. Stroick, Archivum Franciscanum Historicum, 24 (1931), 61, quote by Robin Anne O'Sullivan, 154–55. (This passage is frequently quoted in histories of the beguines).
14. This council also appropriated the Templar's property; exonerated the French king for his actions against the Pope and exacted a tithe for him from the population, ostensibly for a Crusade but actually to fund his war against Flanders; and repressed those orders that defended too radical a practice of poverty. All of this was orchestrated by the French king, Philip the Fair, who had burned Marguerite and dozens of Templars at the stake. It is intriguing to find that the article on beguines and Beghards currently available in the online *Catholic Encyclopedia* (though originally published in 1907) explains the condemnation of the beguines in the Council of Viennes as deriving from their heretical tendencies that "necessitated disciplinary measures, sometimes severe." Ernest Frederick Gilliat-Smith, Beguines & Beghards (1907), in *The Catholic Encyclopedia*, New York: Robert Appleton Company. Retrieved March 17, 2015 from New Advent: http://www.newadvent.org/cathen/02389c.htm. My editor wisely pointed out to me that this article is over one hundred years old and may not express current views, and yet this assumption that "severe" measures against the beguines were necessary remains the standard article on the beguines in the online *Catholic Encyclopedia*, one most readily available by Googling "beguine."

15. Ann L. Barstow, introduction to *A Mirror for Simple Souls*, edited and translated by Charles Crawford, 11.
16. Robert Lerner, preface to *Mirror of Simple Souls*, translated and introduced by Ellen Babinsky, 3.

Chapter 2: I Must Give My Bride, Holy Christianity, a New Cloak

1. Mechthild of Magdeburg, *Flowing Light of the Godhead*, book VI. 21.
2. Ibid., VI.43.
3. Prologue to *Lux Divinitatis* (the Latin translation) and the Middle High German translation, both by Dominican brothers appended to the beginning of Mechthild's manuscript in the Paulist Press version of *Flowing Light of the Godhead.*
4. *Flowing Light of the Godhead.*, VII.13.
5. Ibid., VI.21.
6. She describes a vision in which she sees the reward of the "preachers" in heaven (III.1, 104–5). In "The Six Virtues of St. Dominic," she appreciates his affection, moderation, and mercy as well as his delight in the Holy Spirit and that he taught her that laughing was not wrong (IV.20, 165). IV.21 lists "Sixteen Reasons Why the Order of Preachers Is Dear to God."
7. Ibid., VI.21.
8. Ibid., II.26.
9. Ibid., VII.41
10. Ibid., VII.64.
11. Ibid., VII.6.
12. *Meister Eckhart and the Beguine Mystics: Hadewijch of Brabant, Mechthild of Magdeburg, and Marguerite Porete*, ed. Bernard McGinn (New York, NY: Bloomsbury Academic, 1997), is an excellent analysis of the connections between Eckhart and the beguine.

Chapter 3: Obey No Created Thing except Love

1. Marguerite Porete, *Mirror of Simple Souls*, chap. 4.
2. The *via negativa*, the negative way, is one of the classical methods of talking about God. It proceeds by thinking about ways in which God transcends language (Aquinas: "We cannot know what God is, only what God is not." *Summa Theologica*, question 3). Together with analogy, metaphor, and other approaches, the negative way reminds us that divine reality transcends our words and concepts. Like Pseudo-Dionysius and other great practitioners of the negative way, Marguerite weaves together the names of God, especially love, with a sense of divine mystery.
3. See, for example, Maria Lichtmann's essay, "Marguerite Porete and Meister Eckhart: *The Mirror for Simple Souls* Mirrored," in *Meister Eckhart and the Beguine Mystics*, ed. McGinn, 67
4. Robin Anne O'Sullivan has a helpful description of the teaching context of the beguines in "The School of Love: Marguerite Porete's *Mirror of Simple Souls*," *Journal of Medieval History*, vol. 32 no. 2 (June 2006): 143–62.
5. Zum Brunn and Epiney-Burgard, *Women Mystics of Medieval Europe*, xv.
6. I had the supreme honor of discussing Marguerite's negative theology with His Holiness, the Dalai Lama. He was impressed by her, finding it a Christian parallel to the wisdom of emptiness.
7. *Mirror of Simple Souls*, 31.
8. Ibid.

9. Ibid. Teresa of Avila and John of the Cross also describe their writings in similar terms. Teresa in particular writes about her frustration with male teachers and confessors who cannot take her seriously and wish to impose on her their theology of suffering and atonement. John of the Cross is at pains to interpret the contemplative path as one completely surrounded and upheld by God's endless love. Instead of the self-loathing and anxiety inflicted by institutional authorities, he insisted that nothing in God reflects anger, wrath, or a desire for human suffering.
10. Ibid, 53.
11. Suzanne Kocher analyzes Marguerite's use of gender as an allegory in "Gender in the Religious Allegory of Love: From Active Women to Passive Souls," *Allegories of Love in Marguerite Porete's* Mirror of Simple Souls.
12. The story is told in fascinating detail in Sean Field, *The Beguine, the Angel, and the Inquisitor*. The transcript of her trial and execution is generously translated and posted online by Richard Barton and available at www.uncg.edu/~rebarton/margporete.htm.
13. *Mirror of Simple Souls*, 68.
14. Ibid., 6.
15. Ibid., 7.
16. Ibid., 9.
17. Introduction to *Mirror of Simple Souls*, translated by Edmund Colledge, J. C. Marler, and Judith Grant, p. lxxxvi–vii.
18. Anne L. Barstow, introduction to *A Mirror for Simple Souls*, edited and translated by Charles Crawford, 10.
19. It is possible she knew Boethius's work. In any case, the similarity of genre is all the more striking in light of their shared fate. Boethius wrote his famous text, the *Consolation of Philosophy*, while in prison awaiting execution.
20. These two phrases begin the first and second chapters, respectively, of Julian of Norwich's *Showings*.

Chapter 4: I Saw No Wrath Anywhere

1. Julian of Norwich, "A Revelation of Love," chap. 46. Quotations from Julian are all my translations from *The Writings of Julian of Norwich: A Vision Showed to a Devout Woman and A Revelation of Love*. Nicholas Watson and Jacqueline Jenkins, Editors. Unless otherwise indicated, they are from "A Revelation of Love," which is also known as the Long Text. Her text is often referred to simply as "Showings," which is another way of translating "Revelation." This is the way Colledge and Walsh translate it in their Paulist Press edition of her work. More recently Father John-Julian has produced *The Complete Julian of Norwich*, with both the Short Text (aka "A Vision Showed to a Devout Woman") and the Long Text (aka "A Revelation of Love), together with helpful interpretative and historical essays.
2. Grace Jantzen, *Julian of Norwich*, 15.
3. Thomas Merton, *Conjectures of a Guilty By-Stander*, 191–92, repeated in *The Ways of the Christian Mystics*, 112.
4. Quoted in Father John-Julian, *The Complete Julian of Norwich*, 2. Watson and Jenkins include a long list and analysis of her influence on other writers, including this one, *The Writings of Julian of Norwich*, 10–24, in which Watson and Jenkins make available a highly readable version of her Middle English text.
5. Father John-Julian, *The Complete Julian of Norwich*, 2.
6. Her description of her illness occurs in *Revelation*, chap. 3.

7. Ibid., chap. 2.
8. Ibid., chap. 2. This whole summary of her prayer for three wounds is from chap. 2.
9. For those interested in dialogue with Buddhism, it is interesting to notice resonance with the four "sights" of the Buddha that provoked his quest for enlightenment: suffering in the forms of sickness, aging, and death, and then a monk, who symbolized an antidote to suffering.
10. Mavis Mate, *Women in Medieval English Society*, 73.
11. *Revelation*, chap. 28.
12. Descriptions of the life of an anchoress are described in many places, including John-Julien, *The Complete Julian of Norwich*, 38–44; Jantzen, *Julian of Norwich*, 28–48; Bauerschmidt, *Julian of Norwich*, 210–11. The root text from which they all draw is the *Ancrene Wisse*, a medieval text written to provide detailed guidance to anchoresses.
13. *Revelation*, chap. 10.
14. *The Complete Julian of Norwich*, 381–84.
15. See Jane F. Maynard's *Transfiguring Loss: Julian of Norwich as a Guide for Survivors of Traumatic Grief*, which interprets Julian's theology in light of her identity as herself a survivor of trauma and grief.
16. Shelly Rambo, "Julian of Norwich." *Empire: The Christian Tradition: New Readings of Classical Theologians.*
17. *Vision Showed to a Devout Women*, (aka Short Text), chap. 15.
18. Ibid., chap. 20.
19. *Revelation*, chap. 86.

Chapter 5: "Her God-Hunting Heart"

1. Mechthild of Magdeburg, *Flowing Light of the Godhead*, V.4, 182.
2. Gregory of Nyssa, *From Glory to Glory*, 178–79.
3. Pseudo-Dionysius, *Divine Names*, IV 696A.
4. Ibid, IV 708B.
5. *Flowing Light of the Godhead*, VII.62.
6. Ibid., VII. 16.
7. Ibid., I.18.
8. Ibid., I.19.
9. Joseph Hart, "Come Ye Sinners," *Glory to God* (Louisville, KY: Westminster John Knox Press, 2013), 415.
10. *Flowing Light of the Godhead*, I.1.
11. Ibid., III.9.
12. Ibid.
13. Ibid.
14. Ibid.
15. Theologically inclined readers may be interested in Paul Tillich's lovely little book describing the interdependence of divine powers: *Love, Power and Justice*.
16. Jesus "emptied himself, taking the form of a slave, being born in human likeness" (Phil. 2:7).
17. *Flowing Light of the Godhead*, I.19.
18. Ibid, VII.48. In this scene, Mechthild is restless in the night, troubled by illness and pain. She sees divine love revealed as an empress, white and rosy as in the bloom of youth. Mechthild welcomes her, thanking her for the honor she bestows on the soul, serving it as though the soul were the empress.

19. "I am carrying your sufferings." Ibid., IVV.11.
20. *Mirror of Simple Souls*, chap. 90.
21. Ibid., chap. 122.
22. Ibid., chap. 91.
23. "These people have the highest and gentlest constitution. That is, they are sanguine and choleric rather than melancholy and phlegmatic." Ibid., 99. Marguerite is using the medieval medical model based on the four humors. She means that spiritual endeavors require a great deal of energy and passion; being too inward or depressed undermine the vitality and courage that is required.
24. Ibid., chap. 122.
25. Ibid., chap. 97.
26. Ibid.
27. Julian of Norwich, *Revelation*, chap. 81.
28. Ibid., chap. 67.
29. Ibid., chap. 75.

Chapter 6: "I Have Desired You since the World's Beginning"

1. *Flowing Light of the Godhead*, VII.16.
2. This is a paraphrase of a longer quotation from nineteenth-century reformer Theodore Parker, whose words were used in churches and sermons by Christians and Jews. It was made famous by Martin Luther King's 1964 baccalaureate sermon at Wesleyan University.
3. *Flowing Light of the Godhead*, I. Prologue.
4. Ibid., I.24.
5. In Luke 10:42 Jesus defends Mary who has "chosen the better part" by listening at his feet while Martha is irritated that she is left doing all the work.
6. *Flowing Light of the Godhead*, I.2.
7. This conversion of the soul is also described in a later century by Friar John of Bonilla, "Draw near to Him, not that His Majesty may convert Himself into you, but that He may change you into Himself," *Pax Animae* (Peace of the Soul), chap. 8, *Treatise on Prayer and Mediation*, Peter of Alcantara, 191. (Friar John's lovely treatise was once thought to have been written by St. Peter and was included in this volume of his writings).
8. *Flowing Light of the Godhead*, VI.10.
9. Ibid., I.22.
10. Ibid., 1.44.
11. Ibid., 1.35.
12. Ibid., 1.44. We will see this argument with Reason again in Marguerite's writings.
13. Ibid.
14. There is a good deal of contemporary literature attending to the spiritual dimensions of mind. The literature arising from the centering prayer movement is very good at explaining the theory and practice of meditation as an opening of the mind so it can rest in God. Father Thomas Keating, Basil Pennington, Cynthia Bourgeault, and James Finley are good examples of this literature.
15. Martin Laird, *Into the Silent Land*, p. 1.
16. *Flowing Light of the Godhead*, I.44.
17. Ibid., VI.36.
18. Ibid., VII.1.

Chapter 7: "The Son of God Robbed Me of My Strictest Justice"

1. Mechthild of Magdeburg, *Flowing Light of the Godhead*, VII.1.
2. Ibid., III.4.
3. Ibid., VII.48.
4. Ibid., I.25.
5. Ibid., III.5.
6. Ibid., III.5.
7. Ibid., VII.53.
8. Ibid., VII.53.
9. Ibid., VII.28.
10. Ibid., VII.62.
11. Ibid.
12. Ibid., VI.16.
13. Ibid., III.24.
14. Ibid., II.14.
15. Ibid., II.24.
16. Ibid., II.25.
17. Ibid., V.4, p. 182.
18. Cynthia Bourgeault's *Chanting the Psalms*, the Taizé chants, even "Christian yoga" are examples of a revitalization of bodily spiritual practices.
19. *Flowing Light of the Godhead*, V.8.
20. Ibid., III.21.
21. Ibid., II.8.
22. Ibid., II.8.
23. Ibid. This encounter follows by only five chapters her description of the Trinity's decision to create and then redeem humanity, which was discussed in the previous chapter.
24. Ibid., III.15.
25. Ibid., VII.21.

Chapter 8: "A Virile Vassal in Battle"

1. Mechthild of Magdeburg, *Flowing Light of the Godhead*, II.19.
2. Grace Jantzen was one of the first to criticize the spiritualization of contemplative theology (and its dismissal as feminine, emotional, etc.) in her wonderful book *Power, Gender, and Christian Mysticism*.
3. See Walter Simons, *Cities of Ladies*, 14.
4. *Flowing Light of the Godhead*, VI.16.
5. Ibid., V.31. A lingering association of pleasure with godlessness is even seen in such simple things as the southern tendency to name delicious things after the devil (deviled eggs, devil's food cake)—on the assumption that anything that good can only come from the demonic realms.
6. Ibid., I.l.
7. Ibid., III.9.
8. Ibid., VII.1
9. Ibid.
10. Ibid., VII.5.
11. Ibid., VI.30.
12. Ibid., VI.1.
13. Ibid.
14. Ibid.

15. Ibid.
16. Ibid., V.35.
17. Ibid., VII.28.
18. Many examples could be given. Peter of Alcantara, one of Teresa of Avila's spiritual directors, makes a somewhat similar point in his little handbook on prayer. He emphasizes the importance of love and directs the person to pray to "the very center of his soul, where is the image of God. Let him hearken to Him . . . or as though he gazed upon Him present within his own heart." "Counsels to be Followed in Holy Exercise," *Treatise on Prayer and Meditation*, 115.
19. *Flowing Light of the Godhead*, VI.4.
20. Ibid., IV.3
21. Ibid., IV.2.
22. Ibid., II.24.
23. Ibid., V.34.
24. Ibid.
25. Ibid., VII.34; cf Mechthild sees Jesus in the guise of a pilgrim, coming from Jerusalem, by which he means Christianity, we are told. "I have been driven from my shelter. The heathens do not acknowledge me, Jews do not want me, Christians attack me." Ibid., VII.13. Hopefully, in our own time, we are not so dismissive of other faiths; but for Mechthild to imply that Christianity was no better than heathenism or Judaism would have been a very strong condemnation.
26. Ibid., VII.39, II.19, (et al.), VI.21.
27. Ibid., III.21.
28. Ibid., VII.41.
29. Ibid., IV.3.
30. Ibid., I.46.
31. Ibid., I.44.
32. Ibid.

Chapter 9: "Love Overmastered Me"

1. Marguerite Porete, *Mirror of Simple Souls*, chap. 93.
2. This understanding of theology as transformative wisdom was ancient. Pseudo-Dionysius begins the *Divine Names* by orienting his readers to the power granted by the Spirit "by which, in a manner surpassing speech and knowledge, we reach a union superior to anything available to us by way of our own abilities or activities in the realm of discourse or of intellect" (chap.1 585B–588A). Marguerite's sources would share this "sapiential" understanding of theology. But she lived in a time when theology was quickly becoming the "scientific" (in the older sense) thinking of scholasticism. To get a feel for this contrast, you might read a page from William of St. Thierry and then one from Thomas Aquinas. The doctors at the University of Paris who condemned her writing would all be scholastic theologians.
3. *Mirror of Simple Souls*, prologue, chap. 1.
4. Ibid., chap. 84.
5. Ibid., explicit.
6. Ibid., chap. 2.
7. Ibid., chap. 3.
8. Ibid., chap. 2.
9. Ibid., chap. 1. The longing for God who never quite appears is almost excruciatingly painful. This enflaming desire for God, fluctuating between ravishing

ecstasies and desolating absence, is a common motif in the writings of Hadewijch and Mechthild.

10. Ibid., chap. 1.
11. Marguerite's emphasis on the mediated nature of knowledge of God and the dangers of clinging to images got her in trouble, but it is simply an acknowledgment of the second of the Ten Commandments: "You shall not make for yourself an idol, whether in the form of anything that is in heaven above, or that is on the earth beneath, or that is in the water under the earth" (Exod. 20:4).
12. Interpreting the meaning of the passion has preoccupied the church since its inception. The early church did not think of the passion as a violent death demanded by an angry God. They attributed that kind of violence to Satan and insisted God would never accomplish God's ends by violent means. See, for example, Irenaeus, *Against Heresies* 5.1.1 or Gregory of Nyssa, *Great Catechism* chaps. 21–24.
13. *Mirror of Simple Souls*, chap. 69.
14. Ibid., chap. 31.
15. Ibid., chap. 96.
16. Marguerite uses this analogy in chap. 3.
17. Ibid., chap. 85.
18. Ibid., chap. 19.
19. Ibid.
20. Ibid., chap. 69.
21. Ibid.
22. Ibid. Like the "donkeys of reason" who believe worship can only occur in certain prescribed places, the woman at the well contrasts worship on the mountain with worship in Jerusalem. Jesus counters: "But the hour is coming, and is now here, when the true worshipers will worship the Father in spirit and truth, for the Father seeks such as these to worship him. God is spirit, and those who worship him must worship in spirit and truth" (John 4:23–24).
23. Ibid.
24. Pseudo-Dionysius provides one of many examples of Christianity's appreciation of the majestic transcendence of divine goodness. "Just as the sense can neither grasp nor perceive the things of the mind . . . beings are surpassed by the infinity beyond being, intelligences by the oneness which is beyond intelligence. Indeed, the inscrutable One is out of the reach of every rational process . . . Cause of all existence, and therefore itself transcending existence, it alone could give an authoritative account of what it really is." Pseudo-Dionysius, *Divine Names* I.1 558B.
25. Suzanne Kocher, *Allegories of Love in Marguerite Porete's* Mirror of Simple Souls, 69–79.
26. *Mirror of Simple Souls*, chap. 21.
27. Ibid, chap. 77.

Chapter 10: "The Divine School Is Held with Mouth Closed"

1. Marguerite Porete, *Mirror of Simple Souls*, chap. 66 (paraphrased).
2. Ibid., chap. 8.
3. Ibid.
4. Ibid., chap. 117.
5. In a later century, John of the Cross will make a similar distinction in his spiritual classic, *The Dark Night of the Soul*. The dark night of sense is the asceticism

that overcomes ordinary attachment to physical pain and pleasure. But the more difficult dark night is of the soul when one renounces every trace of conceptual understanding and spiritual pleasure or desire in order to become naked to the nothingness of divine love.

6. Teresa of Avila shares this idea as well. Rather than thinking of sin as pride or lust she describes it as "cowardice, pusillanimity and fear" and attributes lack of self-confidence and self-respect to demonic temptation rather than genuine humility. *Interior Castle*, First Mansion, chap. II.
7. *Mirror of Simple Souls*, chap. 9.
8. Ibid., chap. 8.
9. Ibid., chap. 39.
10. Ibid., chap. 119.
11. Ibid.
12. Ibid., chap 53.
13. Ibid., chap 53.
14. Ibid.
15. John of the Cross is a later contemplative theologian who emphasizes the necessity for reason to descend into darkness: "This dark contemplation must first purge and annihilate it of its natural light and bring it actually into obscurity. It is fitting that this darkness last as long as is necessary for the expulsion and annihilation of the intellect's habitual way of understanding which was a long time in use, and that the divine light and illumination take place." *The Dark Night*, book II 9.3. "As a result the soul must first be set in emptiness and poverty of spirit and purged of every natural support, consolation, and apprehension,—earthly and heavenly. Thus empty, it is truly poor in spirit and stripped of the old man, and thereby able to live that new and blessed life which is the union with God, attained by means of this night." Ibid, book II 9.4.
16. *Mirror of Simple Souls*, chap. 82.
17. Ibid.
18. Cf. ibid., chap. 68.
19. Ibid., chap. 85.
20. Shankara, quoted in Stephen Mithcell, *The Enlightened Mind*, 52.
21. Philo of Alexander, quoted in *The Enlightened Mind*, 25.
22. *Mirror of Simple Souls*, chap. 86.
23. Ibid.
24. Ibid., chap. 87.
25. Ibid.
26. Ibid., chap. 119.

Chapter 11: "This Gift Slays My Thoughts"

1. Marguerite Porete, *Mirror of Simple Souls*, chap. 91.
2. For those interested in theology, *Divine Empathy* by Edward Farley (yes, my father) is an excellent analysis of Christian theology, indicating ways in which very different approaches and methods share this basic awareness of the transcendence of God.
3. These are metaphors drawn from other negative or mystical theologians: Plotinus, Pseudo-Dionysius, Nicholas of Cusa, John of the Cross, the anonymous author of the *Cloud of Unknowing*. The list could be expanded to include many others.

4. Again, this point is made by many other Christian theologians. Nicholas of Cusa explores this theme extensively in "On the Vision of God," in which God is known only on the other side of the wall of reason in which dwells "the coincidence of opposites." John of the Cross quotes 1 John to explain the unity of the soul and God: "'We know we shall be like Him' [I John 3:2], not because the soul will have the same capacity as God—this is impossible—but because all that it is will become like God. Thus it will be called, and shall be, God through participation." *The Dark Night*, book II, 20.5.
5. *Mirror of Simple Souls*, chap. 99.
6. Ibid., chaps. 98, 99.
7. Marguerite is not the only one to lay out the contemplative path as a series of stages. Some two hundred years later, Teresa of Avila will describe the seven rooms of the interior castle as a gradual progression toward union with the Bridegroom. Closer to home, Beatrice of Nazareth (a Cistercian convent in Lier in what is now Belgium, close to Marguerite's home) was the first person to describe the ascent to God in a vernacular language, *The Seven Degrees of Love*, produced sometime before her death in 1268. A brief biography and selections of her work can be found in Fiona Bowie, ed., *Beguine Spirituality*.
8. The summary of these stages occurs in chapter 118, but their meaning spirals through the entire text.
9. *The Way of the Bodhisattva* by Shantideva is a classical source that advocates compassion as the basis of the desire for enlightenment.
10. "And it seems to her that even if she lived a thousand years, her power would be taken up fully with keeping these commandments." *Mirror of Simple Souls*, chap. 118.
11. Ibid.
12. *Mirror of Simple Souls*, chap. 133.
13. John of the Cross spends a good deal of time on this issue. Most of *The Ascent of Mount Carmel* is a description of various kinds of religious experience and why one should not be attached to them. *The Dark Night* is a more concise account of contemplative experience and the necessity of renouncing the practices and experiences that had fed one at an earlier stage.
14. John of the Cross notes that there is a front staircase and a back staircase to God. The back staircase is not very eventful or ecstatic. It is the steady commitment to God practiced over the course of a lifetime. Both ways bring one to the same place. In other words, having or not having ecstasies is not really relevant. He was somewhat critical of Teresa of Avila's ecstasies.
15. In *The City of God* Augustine reflects on existential nothingness at the heart of created being as the cause of the fall. The fallen angels fall because of their irrational pride but also because God withheld from them assurance of their persisting in bliss and they were therefore afraid. In a certain sense, it was this fear in which they "hovered uncertainly" between hope and fear, which caused their fall (Book XI.11). Augustine sees this, but it interrupts the logic of punishment, which for him is essential for making evil make sense, and so he looks at it and then turns away. Paul Tillich's discussion of the threat of radical nonbeing in *The Courage to Be* echoes this point that awareness of the threat of nonbeing is the existential root of human vulnerability.
16. This is what Augustine or Luther are talking about when they say that humanity has turned from God to themselves. They think of this turn in moralistic terms. It is the heart of original sin. It is actually just the natural way created

beings work, but from a religious point of view it is also what separates us from that part of us created for intimacy with God. These theologians are right to identify this as the basic structure of original sin. But to add onto that the myth that it deserves endless punishment seems at odds with the goodness of creation and of God.

17. Quoted by Joe Achenbach, "Star Power," *Smithsonian*, March 2014, vol. 44, no. 11, p. 70. Sagan was an atheist and drew different conclusions from this insight. But it is similar not only to Marguerite's fifth stage but also to Julian of Norwich's image of all creation as something as tiny as a hazelnut precariously hanging on the edge of nothingness.
18. *Mirror of Simple Souls*, chap. 118.
19. This image crops up in contemplative writings. John of the Cross also used the image of wood transforming into fire: "the soul is purged and prepared for union with the divine light just as the wood is prepared for transformation into fire . . . by heating and enkindling it from without, the fire transforms the wood into itself and makes it as beautiful as it is itself. Once transformed, the wood no longer has any activity or passivity of its own." *The Dark Night*, book II, chap. 10.1.
20. *Mirror of Simple Souls*, chap. 118.The word Marguerite is using here is *vouloir*, to want, wish, or desire. It is often translated as will or as inclination. She seems to mean a little of both. One must desire what God desires in such a way that one is able to will to renounce desire.
21. Ibid., chap. 118.
22. Meister Eckhart, sermon 4, "True Hearing."
23. *Mirror of Simple Souls*, chap. 2. The sixth stage concludes with the assurance that Love has paid her "debt," presumably an allusion to the promise stated in chapter 2. The metaphor of debt may be an allusion to Anselm's substitutionary atonement, which relied on debt to interpret Christ's sacrifice. Here, however, the debt is what Love owes to humanity and the debt is paid, not in blood, but in the presentation of the path to union.
24. Ibid., chap. 118.
25. Ibid., chap. 76.
26. Ibid., chap. 121.
27. Ibid., chap. 122.

Chapter 12: "Who Shall Teach Me What I Need to Know"

1. Julian of Norwich, *Revelation*, chap. 50.
2. Ibid., chap. 10.
3. Ibid., chap. 5.
4. Ibid. There is an old gospel song, "Two Cloaks," that uses a somewhat similar image.
5. Ibid., chap. 53, cf. 58.
6. Ibid., chap. 54.
7. Ibid., chap. 56.
8. Ibid., chap. 57.
9. Ibid., chap. 51.
10. Ibid., chap. 6.
11. Ibid., chap. 46.
12. Ibid., chap. 39.
13. Ibid., chap. 38, 39.
14. Ibid., chap. 11.

15. Ibid., chap. 32.
16. Ibid. Watson notes in his comments that William Langland (the author of the contemporaneous *Piers Plowman*) also puts in the mouth of Christ the assurance that he can do mercy wherever he wishes, even if Scripture says otherwise. Both Langland and Julian allude to Luke 18:26–27, in which the disciples ask in dismay who can be saved, and Jesus answers: "What is impossible to mortals is possible for God." This echoes also Isaiah 55, in which God assures the prophet that God can save those who seem unforgivable because "my thoughts are not your thoughts, nor are your ways my ways. . . . So shall my word be that goes out from my mouth; it shall not return to me empty, but it shall accomplish that which I purpose. . . . For you shall go out in joy, and be led back in peace" (Isa. 55: 8, 11, 12).
17. *Revelation*, chap. 50.
18. Ibid., chap. 45.
19. Ibid., chap. 51.
20. Ibid., chap. 86. The chronology of how she came to interpret her visions is not the same as the narrative of her text. She uses this assurance, which she received fifteen years after her illness and vision, as the conclusion of her text. The parable of the lord and servant was given to her in the initial vision and occurs about two thirds of the way through the Long Text, but she indicates she only came to understand it twenty years later.
21. Ibid., chap. 51.
22. Ibid. This twofold sense of creation, in which humanity is sinlessly knit to the Trinity but subject to sin through embodiment, is taken up systematically in subsequent chapters.
23. This *felix culpa* (happy fault) was part of the services of Holy Weeks from as early as the seventh century, if not before.
24. *Revelation*, chap. 22.
25. This understanding of the fall as a necessary element of the redemption of humanity is a version of what John Hick identifies as the Irenaean theodicy, named for the third-century theologian Irenaeus, who made a similar argument (*Evil and the God of Love*). This ancient way of thinking about human sin and suffering was overshadowed by Augustine's emphasis on pride and the inexplicable perversity and guilt of the fall. But it never entirely died out. It is there in the lovely letter of John Keats to his siblings (http://www.mrbauld.com/keatsva.html), in Schleiermacher, Tillich, Martin Buber, and many contemporary thinkers.
26. *Revelation*, chap. 51.
27. Ibid., chap. 10.

Chapter 13: Mother, Father, Spouse

1. Julian of Norwich, *Revelation*, chap. 52.
2. Ibid., chap. 2.
3. See Virginia Ramey Mollenkott's *The Divine Feminine: Biblical Imagery of God as Female* and Carolyn Walker Bynum, *Jesus as Mother*.
4. Though it is impossible to know, I have wondered if her emphasis on divine motherhood does not suggest that she herself was a mother. In my experience, people who are not mothers are not especially interested in motherhood, and they do not know enough about it to consider how its different elements could reflect divine goodness and power.
5. *Revelation*, chap. 59.

6. Ibid., chap. 60. The following sentences paraphrase the rest of her paragraph.
7. Ibid.
8. Ibid., chap. 58.
9. Ibid.
10. Ibid.
11. Ibid.
12. Ibid., chap. 63.
13. Ibid., chap. 61.
14. Ibid., chap. 60.
15. Ibid., chap. 24.
16. Ibid., chap. 60.
17. Ibid., chap. 59.
18. Ibid., chap. 61
19. Ibid., chap. 63
20. Ibid., chap. 58.
21. Ibid., chap. 1.
22. Ibid., chap. 86.
23. The literal meaning of "perichoresis," the word often used to describe the unity and diversity of the Trinity, is to dance around.
24. For example, "the friendliness of the Father," chap. 8; "to comfort and cheer his dear-worthy friends," chap. 14.
25. Ibid., chap. 7.
26. Ibid.
27. Ibid., chap. 6.
28. Father John-Julian cites possible sources, including the sixth-century Pseudo Dionysius's *The Complete Julian of Norwich* (p. 392). Watson and Jenkins allude to what they take to be her Neoplatonic sense of creation flowing out from God; *The Writings of Julian of Norwich* (p. 162).
29. *Revelation*, chap. 11.
30. Ibid.
31. Ibid.
32. Wendy Farley, *Tragic Vision and Divine Compassion: A Contemporary Theodicy*.
33. Ibid., chap. 75.

Chapter 14: The Fairest Face in Heaven

1. Julian of Norwich, *Revelation*, chap. 10.
2. Shelly Rambo describes her attention to wounds as an "imperative to witness wounds and to resist the powers that cover the wounds and deny their reality," 183.
3. *Revelation*, chap. 4.
4. Ibid., chap. 66. Beginning with chapter 66, the chapters are numbered differently in different translations. I am following Watson and Jenkin's *Writings of Julian of Norwich* and Colledge and Walsh's *Showings*.
5. Ibid., chap. 67.
6. Ibid., chap. 68.
7. Ibid., chap. 67.
8. Ibid., chap. 86.
9. Ibid., chap. 77.
10. Ibid., chap. 73.
11. C. S. Lewis provides a contemporary version of the ancient ransom theory of atonement in his children's novel, *The Lion, the Witch, and the Wardrobe*.

12. *Revelation*, chap. 50.
13. Ibid., chap. 1. This is actually the title of the *Revelation of Love* (aka the Long Text).
14. Ibid., chap. 22
15. Ibid., chap. 21.
16. Ibid.
17. Ibid., chap. 22.
18. Ibid., chap. 27.
19. Ibid., chap. 24. This is one of the places she adds "that shall be saved." What this means is the question that this chapter is wrestling with.
20. Ibid., chap. 51.
21. Ibid., chap. 62. This point is echoed later when Jesus reminds her that the fiend is overcome by the passion: "And all this teaching and true comfort applies generally to all Christians, as was said before and is God's desire." Ibid., chap. 68.
22. Father John-Julian discusses this in his appendix to the *Complete Julian*, as well as elsewhere. He quotes her acceptance of the doctrine of hell in chapters 32 and 33. However, this is precisely what generates the long conversation between her and Jesus on this point that culminates in the exemplum of the lord and servant and the theology of divine motherhood. The last chapters of her book (52–86) draw out the implications of her theology for spiritual practice. Chief among the sins she attributes to spiritual people is the fear of divine anger and lack of faith in the divine love.
23. *Revelation*, chap. 5.
24. Ibid., chap. 13. The following discussion is drawn primarily from this chapter.
25. Ibid., chap. 73.
26. Ibid., chap. 12.
27. Ibid., chap. 85.
28. Ibid., chap. 75.

Conclusion

1. Walter Simons, *Cities of Ladies*, 143.
2. Julian of Norwich, *Revelation*, chap. 64.
3. Mechthild of Magdeburg, *Flowing Light of the Godhead*, IV.12.
4. Beverly Lanzetta, *Radical Wisdom*, 121.
5. Cynthia Bourgeault, *Centering Prayer and Inner Awakening*, 97.
6. Bourgeault, *The Meaning of Mary Magdalene: Discovering the Woman at the Heart of Christianity*, 218.
7. Julian of Norwich, *Revelation*, chap. 2.
8. *Meaning of Mary Magdalene*, 217 (emphasis in original).

Bibliography

Achenback, Joe. "Star Power." *Smithsonian* 44, no. 11 (March 2014).

Aelred of Rievaulx. *Treatises and Pastoral Prayer: Treatises: On Jesus at the Age of Twelve, Rule of Life for a Recluse, and the Pastoral Prayer.* Kalamazoo, MI: Cistercian Publications, 1971.

Aquinas, Thomas. *Summa Theologia. Volume I.* Complete English Edition in Five Volumes. Translated by Fathers of the English Dominican Province. Westminster, MD: Christian Classics, 1981.

Arblaster, John, and Rob Faesen, "The Influence of Beatrice of Nazareth on Marguerite Porete: the Seven Manners of Love Revised." *Journal of Historical Studies* 61:41–88.

Augustine. *City of God.* Translated by Henry Bettenson. Introduction by David Knowles. New York: Penguin Book, 1972.

Barstow, Ann L. Introduction to *A Mirror for Simple Souls.* Edited and translated by Charles Crawford. New York: Crossroad Spiritual Classics, 1990.

Barton, Richard, trans. *The Trial of Marguerite Porete (1310).* Translated from Henry Charles Lea. *A History of the Inquisition of the Middle Ages,* 3 vols. New York: Macmillan, 1922) 2:575–578.

Bauerschmidt, Frederick Christian. *Julian of Norwich and the Mystical Body Politic of Christ.* Notre Dame, IN: University of Notre Dame Press, 1995.

Boethius. *Consolation of Philosophy.* Translated by Victor Watts. New York: Penguin Press, 2000.

Bondi, Roberta. *To Love as God Loves.* Minneapolis: Fortress Press, 1987.

Bourgeault, Cynthia. *Centering Prayer and Inner Awakening.* Cambridge, MA: Cowley Publications, 2004.

———. *Chanting the Psalms: A Practical Guide with Instructional CD.* Boston: New Seeds, 2006.

———. *The Meaning of Mary Magdalene: Discovering the Woman at the Heart of Christianity.* Boston: Shambhala Publications, 2010.

Bowie, Fiona, ed. *Beguine Spirituality: Mystical Writings of Mechthild of Magdeburg, Beatrice of Nazareth, and Hadewijch of Brabant.* Translated by Oliver Davies. New York: Crossroad, 1990.

Brown, Peter. *The Body and Society: Men, Women and Sexual Renunciation in Early Christianity*. 2nd ed. New York: Columbia University Press, 2008.

Burgtorf, Jochen, Paul F. Crawford, and Helen H. Nicholson, ed. *The Debate on the Trial of the Templars (1307–1314)*. Surrey, England: Ashgate Publishing, 2010.

Bynum, Caroline Walker. *Holy Feast, Holy Fast: Religious Significance of Food to Medieval Women*. Berkeley, CA: University of California Press, 1987.

———. *Jesus as Mother: Studies in the Spirituality of the High Middle Ages*. Berkeley, CA: University of California Press, 1982.

Charlton, James. *Non-Dualism in Eckhart, Julian of Norwich and Traherne: A Theopoetic Reflection*. New York: Bloomsbury, 2013

Conn, Marie A. *Noble Daughters: Unheralded Women in Western Christianity, 13th to 18th Centuries*. Westport, CT: Greenwood Press, 2000.

Cre, Marleen. "Women in the Charterhouse? Julian of Norwich's *Revelations of Divine Love* and Marguerite Porete's *Mirror of Simple Souls* in British Library, MS Additional 37790." In *Writing Religious Women: Female Spiritual and Textual Practices in Late Medieval England*. Edited by Denis Renevey and Christiania Whitehead, 43–55. Toronto: University of Toronto Press, 2000.

Dronke, Peter. *Women Writers of the Middle Ages: A Critical Study of Texts from Perpetua (203) to Marguerite Porete (1310)*. Cambridge: Cambridge University Press, 1984.

Farley, Wendy. *Tragic Vision, Divine Compassion: A Contemporary Theodicy*. Louisville, KY: Westminster John Knox Press, 1990.

Field, Sean L. *The Beguine, the Angel, and the Inquisitor: The Trials of Marguerite Porete and Guiard of Cressonessart*. Notre Dame, IN: Notre Dame University Press, 2012.

Finley, James. *Christian Meditation: Experiencing the Presence of God*. New York: HarperOne, 2005.

Gilliat-Smith, Frederick Ernest. "Beguines & Beghards." In *The Catholic Encyclopedia*. New York: Robert Appleton Co., 1907. Retrieved March 17, 2015 from New Advent: http://www.newadvent.org/cathen/02389c.htm.

Gregory of Nyssa. *From Glory to Glory: Texts from Gregory of Nyssa's Mystical Writings*. Translated by Herbert Musurillo. Crestwood, NY: St. Vladimir's Seminary Press, 1995.

———. "The Great Catechism." In *The Nicene and Post-Nicene Fathers*, series 2. Vol. 5: *Gregory of Nyssa: Dogmatic Treatises, Etc*. Translated and edited by Philip Schaff and Henry Wace, 471–509. Grand Rapids, MI: Eerdmans, 1954.

Guigo II. *Ladder of the Monks and Twelve Meditations*. Translated by Edmund Colledge and James Walsh. Kalamazoo, MI: Cistercian Publications, 1979.

Hadewijch. *The Complete Works*. Translated by Mother Columba Hart, OSB. New York: Paulist Press, 1980.

Hollywood, Amy. *Soul as Virgin Wife: Mechthild of Magdeburg, Marguerite Porete, and Meister Eckhart*. Notre Dame, IN: University of Notre Dame Press, 2001.

Holmes, Emily A. *Flesh Made Word: Medieval Women Mystics, Writing, and the Incarnation*. Waco, TX: Baylor University Press, 2014.

Holmes, Emily, and Wendy Farley. *Women, Writing, Theology: Transforming a Tradition of Exclusion*. Waco, TX: Baylor University Press, 2011.

Jantzen, Grace. *Julian of Norwich: Mystic and Theologian*. New York: Paulist Press, 1987.

———. *Power, Gender, and Christian Mysticism*. Cambridge, England: Cambridge University Press, 1995.

Father John-Julian, OJN. *The Complete Julian of Norwich*. Brewster, MA: Paraclete Press, 2009.

John of the Cross. *The Collected Works of St. John of the Cross*. Translated by Kieran Kavanaugh and Otilio Rodriguez. Washington, DC: Institute of Carmelite Studies, ICS Publications, 1979.

Julian of Norwich. *The Complete Julian of Norwich*. Translation and Essays by Father John-Julian. Brewster, MA: Paraclete Press, 2009.

———. *Showings*. Translated by Edmund Colledge and James Walsh. New York: Paulist Press, 1978.

———. *The Writings of Julian of Norwich: A Vision Showed to a Devout Woman and A Revelation of Love*. Edited by Nicholas Watson and Jacqueline Jenkins. Pennsylvania Park, PA: Pennsylvania State University Press, 2006.

Keating, Thomas. *Open Mind Open Heart: The Contemplative Dimension of the Gospel.* New York: Continuum Publishing Co., 1992.

Keats, John. "Keats on Vale of Soul-Making." Letter to George and Georgiana Keats. May, 1819. www.mrbauld.com/keatsva.html.

Kelly, Joseph. Review of *Literature and Heresy in the Age of Chaucer*, by Andrew Cole, *This Rough Magic*, January 2010, www.thisroughmagic.org/kelly%20review.html.

Kocher, Suzanne. *Allegories of Love in Marguerite of Porete's* Mirror of Simple Souls. Turnhout, Belgium: Brepols Publishers, 2008.

Lahav, Rina. "Marguerite Porete and the Predicament of Her Preaching in Fourteenth-Century France." In *Gender, Catholicism and Spirituality: Women and the Roman Catholic Church in Britain and Europe, 1200–1900*. Edited by Laurence Lux-Sterritt and Carmon M. Mangion, 38–48. New York: Palgrave Macmillan, 2011.

Laird, Martin. *Into the Silent Land: A Guide to the Christian Practice of Contemplation*. Oxford, England: Oxford University Press, 2006.

Lambert, Malcolm. *Medieval Heresy: Popular Movements from the Gregorian Reform to the Reformation*, 2nd ed. Oxford: Blackwell Publishers, Second Edition, 1992.

Lanzetta, Beverly. *Radical Wisdom: A Feminist Mystical Theology*. Minneapolis, MN: Fortress Press, 2005.

Lerner, Robert. Preface to *Mirror of Simple Souls*. Translated by Ellen Babinsky. New York: Paulist Press, 1993.

Lewis, C. S. *The Lion, the Witch, and the Wardrobe*. New York: HarperCollins, 1994.

Lichtmann, Maria. "Marguerite Porete and Meister Eckhart: *The Mirror for Simple Souls* Mirrored." http://www.academia.edu/862355/Marguerite_Porete_and_Meister_Eckhart_The_Mirror_for_Simple_Souls_Mirrored.

Mate, Mavis E. *Women in Medieval English Society*. Cambridge, England: University of Cambridge Press, 1999.

Maynard, Jane F. *Transfiguring Loss: Julian of Norwich as a Guide for Survivors of Traumatic Grief*. Cleveland: Pilgrim Press, 2006.

McGinn, Bernard, ed. *Meister Eckhart and the Beguine Mystics: Hadewijch of Brabant, Mechthild of Magdeburg, and Marguerite Porete*. New York: Bloomsbury Academic, 1997.

———. *Varieties of Vernacular Mysticism*. New York: Crossroad Publishing, 2012.

Mechthild of Magdeburg. *Das Fliessende Licht der Gottheit: Nach der Einsiedler Hand, schrift in kritischem Vergleich mit der gesamten Überlieferung*. Band l Text. Edited by Hans Neumann. Munchen: Artemis Verlag. 1990.

———. *The Flowing Light of the Godhead.* Translated by Frank Tobin. New York: Paulist Press, 1998.

———. *Mechthild of Magdeburg: Selections from the Flowing Light of the Godhead.* Translated by Elizabeth A. Andersen. Cambridge, England: D. S. Brewer, 2003.

Meister Eckhart. *The Essential Sermons, Commentaries, Treatises, and Defense.* Translated by Edmund Colledge and Bernard McGinn. New York: Paulist Press, 1981.

Merton, Thomas. *Conjectures of a Guilty Bystander.* New York: Doubleday Publishing, 1968.

———. *Ways of the Christian Mystics: Essays from Mystics and Zen Masters.* Boston, MA: Shambhala Press, 1994.

Miles, Margaret. *Rereading Historical Theology: Before, During, and After Augustine.* Eugene, Oregon: Cascade Books, 2008.

Miller, Tanya Tabler. "Mirror of the Scholarly (Masculine) Soul: Scholastics, Beguines, and Gendered Spirituality in Medieval Paris." In *Negotiating Clerical Identities: Priests, Monks and Masculinity in the Middle Ages*, edited by Jennifer D. Thibodeaux, 238–56. New York: Palgrave Macmillan, 2010.

Mitchell, Stephen. *The Enlightened Mind: An Anthology of Sacred Prose.* New York, NY: Harper Perennial, 1991

Mollenkott, Virginia Ramey. *The Divine Feminine: Biblical Imagery of God as Female.* Eugene, OR: Wipf and Stock, 2014 (reissued).

Murk-Jansen, Saski. *Brides in the Desert: The Spirituality of the Beguines.* London: Darton, Longman and Todd, 1998.

Musurillo, Herbert, trans."Martyrdom of Saints Perpetua and Felicitas." In *Acts of the Christian Martyrs.* Oxford University Press, 1972. Digitized January 28, 2010.

Newell, John Philip. *A New Harmony: The Spirit, the Earth, and the Human Soul.* San Francisco: Jossey-Bass Publishers, 2011.

O'Sullivan, Robin. "School of Love: Marguerite Porete's *Mirror of Simple Souls.*" *Journal of Medieval History* 32, no. 2, (June 2006): 143–62.

Pennington, M. Basil. *Lectio Divina: Renewing the Ancient Practice of Praying the Scriptures.* New York: Crossroads Publishing Co., 1998.

Peter of Alcantara. *Treatise on Prayer and Meditation.* Translated by Dominic Devas. Charlotte, NC: Tan Books and Publishers, 2009.

Petroff, Elizabeth Alvilda. *Medieval Women's Visionary Literature.* New York: Oxford University Press, 1986.

Porete, Marguerite. *Le mirouer des simples ames.* Corpus Christianorum. Edited by Romana Guarnieri. Continuatio Mediaualis XIX. Turnholti: Typographi Brepols Editores Pontificii, 1986.

———. *The Mirror of Simple Souls.* Translated by Edmund Colledge, OSA, J. C. Marler, and Judith Grant. Notre Dame, IN: University of Notre Dame Press: 1999.

———. *The Mirror of Simple Souls.* Translated by Ellen L. Babinsky. New York: Paulist Press, 1993.

Poor, Sara. *Mechthild of Magdeburg and Her Book: Gender and the Making of Textual Authority.* Philadelphia, PA: University of Pennsylvania Press, 2004.

Pseudo-Dionysius. *The Complete Works.* Translated by Colm Luibheid. Mahwah, NJ: Paulist Press, 1987.

Rambo, Shelly. "Julian of Norwich." In *Empire and the Christian Tradition: New Readings of Classical Theologians.* Edited by Kwok Pui-lan, Don H. Compier, and Joerg Rieger, 167–84. Minneapolis: Fortress Press, 2007.

Rolf, Veronica Mary. *Julian's Gospel: Illuminating the Life and Revelations of Julian of Norwich*. Maryknoll, NY: Orbis Books, 2013.
Ruether, Rosemary Radford. *Visioning Women: Three Medieval Mystics*. Minneapolis, MN: Augsburg Books, 2001.
Shantideva. *The Way of the Bodhisattva (Bodhicaryavatara)*. 2nd ed. Translated by the Padmakara Translation Group. Boston: Shambhala Publications, 2006.
Simons, Walter. *City of Ladies: Beguine Communities in the Medieval Low Countries, 1200–1565*. Philadelphia, PA: University of Pennsylvania Press, 2003.
Stoner, Abby. "Sisters Between: Gender and the Medieval Beguines." Medievalist.net, www.medievalists.net/2013/03/17/sisters-between-gender-and-the-medieval-beguines-2/. Originally published in Ex Post Facto 4, no. 2, (Spring 1995).
Teresa of Avila. *Interior Castle*. Translated by E. Allison Peers. New York: Image Books, Doubleday, 1989.
Tillich, Paul. *The Courage to Be*. 3rd ed. New Haven, CT: Yale University Press, 2014.
———.*Love, Power, and Justice: Ontological Analysis and Ethical Applications*. Oxford, England: Oxford University Press: 1954.
Valentasis, Richard. *Making of the Self: Ancient and Modern Asceticism*. Eugene, OR: Wipf and Stock Publishers, 2008.
Voss-Roberts, Michelle. *Dualities: A Theology of Difference*. Louisville, KY: Westminster John Knox Press, 2010.
Watson, Nicholas. "Melting into God the English Way: Deification in the Middle English Version of Marguerite Porete's *Mirouer des simples âmes anienties*." *Prophets Abroad: The Reception of Continental Holy Women in Late-Medieval England*, edited by Rosalynn Voaden, 18–30. Cambridge, England: D. S. Brewer, 1996.
Williams, Tara. *Inventing Womanhood: Gender and Language in Later Middle English Writing*. Columbus: Ohio State University Press, 2011.
Zum Brunn, Emilie, and Georgette Epiney-Burgard. *Women Mystics in Medieval Europe*. New York: Paragon House, 1998.

CPSIA information can be obtained at www.ICGtesting.com
Printed in the USA
LVOW10s1115281215

468068LV00012B/209/P